Natural Learning and the Natural Curriculum:

'anybody, any age;
any time, any place;
any pathway, any pace'

by Roland Meighan

Educational Heretics Press
in association with
Natural Parent magazine

Published 2001 by Educational Heretics Press
113 Arundel Drive, Bramcote Hills, Nottingham NG9 3FQ

British Cataloguing in Publication Data

Meighan, Roland
        Natural Learning and the Natural Curriculum:
        anybody, any age; any time, any place;
        any pathway, any pace
        1.Learning – Psychology of 2.Learning ability 3.Parenting
        4.Education – Philosophy of
        I.Title
        370.1'5

ISBN   1-900219-19-0

Design and production: Educational Heretics Press

Cover design by Natural Parent magazine

Printed by Esparto, Slack Lane, Derby

Contents

**Part one: Natural learning
    and the natural curriculum**   **1**
1. Natural learners
2. Wanted! A new vocabulary for learning
3. The natural curriculum

Part two: Parents   **13**
1. Reluctant educational heretics
2. Parents as researchers
3. Purposive conversation and effective learning
4. Damage limitation
5. Grandparent power?

Part three: Learners and learning systems   **37**
1. Order! Order!
2. Where does the bully mentality come from?
3. Back to the future?
4. Its not what you learn but the way that you learn it
5. Beans in a jar and the domination of the peer group
6 Instead of fear

Part four: Teachers   **67**
1. What is a good teacher?
2. Crowd instruction: the cop without a uniform
3. Head teachers, leadership and courage

Part five: Superstitions and myths   **77**
1. The superstition of socialisation
2. The superstition of standards
3. Some educational superstitions of our time -Shakespeare,
   Maths and Handwriting
4. Dyslexia and the obsession with literacy
5. You become what you read

Part six: Visions of the next learning system   **97**
1. Teaching tomorrow
2. Roland Meighan interviews Sir Christopher Ball
3. Learning centres instead of schools?

Postscript: 'Boulevard of Broken Dreams'   **116**

Foreword

Ever since Socrates said *"Yes, but. ..."* to his fellow Athenians, it's been clear that the health of any society is judged by those who dare to question the status quo. Numbers of 'nay-sayers' tend to ebb and flow, usually depending on the beheading policy current at the time, but they have always been around as a vital function of the democratic process.

Education is one sector of society to attract more than its fair share of iconoclasts, possibly because it has always proved to be such a rich and reliable seam for those who can see there really must be a better way.

Many of those hail from the United States, but we are particularly fortunate in this country to have Dr Roland Meighan, a friend of the legendary John Holt, and who has taken on the mantle of education's most eloquent critic.

I first came across Roland in the autumn of 1997 when we were launching *Natural Parent*. I was looking for a regular column that would debunk and question conventional education, and the name of Roland Meighan quickly came to the lips of virtually everyone I asked.

He accepted the commission without too much bother, and he didn't ask too many questions. Perhaps he had had his fill of editors over the years who would edit out his more controversial statements, or perhaps 'forget' to publish the article at all, and had assumed I was another of the same ilk. Not so. His first column, which was published in November 1997, was just what I wanted. It was bold, challenging, and laced with both erudition and wit.

And so it has been over the months, and now the years, since then. The standard has not flagged at all, and each column has shown another aspect of Roland's learning and compassion. And that I think is the key to Roland — his compassion for the children who are in our schools.

This book is a compilation of all of those columns, but arranged in a logical way to form a natural progression of the argument. It is, of course, a wonderful book, but it is more than that. It is a radical, possibly revolutionary, book, as well. It will give you courage, if that is what you need, it will give you insight; it will certainly give you food for thought about what we are doing to our children.

Best of all, it comes without my edits (all done in the best possible taste, and always because of space constraints). So on with the unexpurgated Roland — a treat indeed.

Bryan Hubbard
Editor
Natural Parent

Part one: Natural learning

1. Natural learners

Parents soon find out that young children are natural learners. They are like explorers or research scientists busily gathering information and making meaning out of the world. Most of this learning is not the result of teaching, but rather a constant and universal learning activity, as natural as breathing. Our brains are programmed to learn unless discouraged. A healthy brain stimulates itself by interacting with what it finds interesting or challenging in the world around it. It learns from any mistakes and operates a self-correcting process.

We parents achieve the amazing feats of helping our children to talk, walk and make sense of the home and the environment in which it is set, by responding to this natural learning process. All this is achieved, with varying degrees of success, by so-called amateurs – those of us who are parents, along with other care-givers such as grandparents.

The highly sophisticated activity of parents is described as 'dovetailing' into the child's behaviour. Parents, frequently the mothers for the largest share of the time, have no pre-determined plan of language teaching. We simply respond to the cues provided and give support to the next stage of learning as the child decides to encounter it. What we discover as parents is that, if supported and encouraged, children will not only begin to make sense of their world, but can also acquire the attitudes and skills necessary for successful learning throughout their lives.

But, this process of natural learning can be hindered or halted by insensitive adult interference. Sadly, the schools available to us, whether state or private, are often based on an impositional model which, sooner or later, causes children to lose confidence in their natural learning and its self-correcting features, and instead, learn to be dependent on others to 'school' their minds. In the process, most schools manage gradually to transform learning from one of the most rewarding of all human activities into a rather dull, often boring, fragmenting, mind-shrinking, sometimes painful and soul-shrinking experience.

A prize-winning New York teacher, John Taylor Gatto, describes this kind of schooling as training children *"... to be obedient to a script written by remote strangers ... Education demands you write the script of your own life with the help of people who love or care about you."*

The consequence is that parents wanting an effective and morally healthy education for their children based on natural learning principles, are in the same position as people wanting more healthy, vegetarian or vegan diets, or non-smokers wanting clean air in public places, or investors wanting to invest their money in ethical rather than exploitative enterprises, or people wanting to save the environment from further and possibly terminal destruction.

The system is not in the habit of providing any of these things, and often has a vested interest in providing the opposite. So, like the vegetarian pioneers, the non-smoking rights movement and the environmental protection groups, parents wanting education that respects natural learning principles, will have to argue and organise to try to get it.

There are at least three options. One is to find one of the rare examples of humane schools free from domination, (often, but not necessarily, small in size). Ivan Illich describes these as 'convivial' institutions rather than 'coercive' ones.

A second is to fight a rearguard action of damage limitation by deliberately providing alternative learning at home in out of school hours, and maintaining a continuous critical dialogue with children about the schooling experience. Since my son James chose to go to school rather than have home-based education, this was my own path, damage limitation, and a full account follows later in this book. James observed that *'school is a wreck, but I can find bits of treasure in it.'*

A third option is to join the fast-growing minority, (grown from about ten families in England and Wales in 1977 to possibly as many as 50,000 families at present), who undertake home-based education and, increasingly, establish co-operative family learning centres to support their activity.

2. Wanted! A new vocabulary for learning

The September 1998 edition (Vol. 30, No.5) of the *Journal of Curriculum Studies* opens with a powerful article by a leading curriculum theorist, Bill Reid, about 'the end of curriculum'. Previously, *In Place of* Schools (London: New Education Press) was the title of a book by John Adcock, published in 1994, thus declaring the word 'school' redundant. We need, therefore, a new vocabulary to take us into the next learning system. This is not a matter of mere debate but of necessity. The shape of the next learning system has to be described not only in new words to convey the new approach, but also in words that make sense to parents.

But first, the old vocabulary has to go. The first casualty has to be **school**. As a word and concept it has degenerated. It used to mean a **voluntary association of learners asking questions and seeking the truth**. In earlier times, when scholars (or 'schoolers') like Peter Abelard travelled from town to town, an informal school of enquirers would assemble for a dialogue about his radical ideas. Somehow this idea of a voluntary gathering of learners has become debased. In his classic book, *Life in Classrooms*, (Eastbourne: Holt, Rhinehart and Winston, 1968) Philip Jackson concluded that: *"for all the children some of the time, and for some other children all the time, the classroom resembles a cage from which there is no* *escape"*.   We need to remember that when mass compulsory schooling was first adopted in the USA, the children of the pioneer families were escorted to the state establishments by armed soldiers, against the will of the families concerned.   Currently, in the UK it is hailed as an advance that police cars are used to round up any reluctant learners.   The undesirable outcomes are that, somehow, schools have transformed learning from one of the most natural and rewarding of all human activities into a unnatural, fear-laden and often alienating experience.

Next, the word **curriculum** has to go.   It has come to mean an imposed course study so dehumanised that all the key decisions about what to learn, when to learn, and how to learn, have been taken before any of the learners have been met and encountered as people.   At one point in the National Curriculum deliberations, it was suggested that we refer to 'curriculum study units' or CSUs rather than pupils, as a final dehumanisation.   Bill Reid, in his *Journal of Curriculum Studies* piece, declares that this idea of curriculum, as a nationally institutionalised form of education, is now played out.   Even   Prime Minister, Tony Blair, with his somewhat conservative interpretation of 'education, education, education' as being synonymous with 'schooling, schooling, schooling', has stated that,   *"we will move away from a system that assumes every child of a particular age moves at the same pace in every subject, and develop a system directed to the particular talents and interests of every pupil."*

Another word that may have to go is **education**.   Quite a few years ago, Bertrand Russell observed that we were faced with the paradoxical fact that education had become one of the chief obstacles to intelligence and to freedom of thought.   In common usage, education has ceased to mean 'asking questions all the time, questioning answers all the time, and questioning the questions'.   Instead it has become a paper-chase.   When you are asked about your education, you are expected to produce a list of set courses completed and certificates obtained, or name the place of conscription that you were required to attend.

Next, one of officialdom's favourite words may have to go.   It is **standards**.   The idea of standards in education is both ambiguous and subjective. For some it means remembering the information designated as essential by adults in power positions, even though there is little agreement on what is essential. Training students to be good at the shallow learning of selected mechanical tasks enshrined in institutionally imposed syllabuses, does not produce the more important **deep learning**, the kind we already need, and will need more and more in the future.

The first objection to shallow learning systems is that they tend to eradicate the potential to develop deep learning, as the most recent brain activity research shows, on the principle of 'if you do not use it, you lose it'. With the habits of deep learning in your repertoire, you can do shallow learning more or less at will. The reverse, however, does not apply.

Another objection to the current definition of standards, is that most of the required shallow learning is junk knowledge. I define junk knowledge as 'something you did not need or want to know yesterday, do not need or want to know today, and are unlikely to need or want to know tomorrow'. If you do need or want to know it eventually, possessing the deeper knowledge of such things as questioning, researching, evaluating, self direction and self discipline, will enable you to learn it.

So, parents and children will need to un-learn the old vocabulary and learn a new one. The literature on the next learning system has several suggestions for a word to replace school. Some writers talk of open learning centres, or learning studios, or learning pavilions, or learning networks, or community learning sites, or learning cafés. Another option is to refer to centres for personalised education, or CPEs. Others want to retain the word school in revised formulations such as virtual-schools or cyber-schools. For a time I favoured flexi-schooling but generally, the government and its schools proved to be resistant to the idea of becoming flexible.

The main candidate to replace the word curriculum, is the expression 'personal learning plan' or 'personal learning programme'. Personally, I favour retaining the word curriculum as part of the expression, the **catalogue curriculum**. Such a term implies that learners are able to construct their own pattern of learning from a catalogue of ideas and possibilities, including ready-made courses, individualised courses, and learning co-operatives - groups of learners who want to work democratically and design their own courses.

To replace the word education, many writers now favour referring to 'learning', or 'lifelong learning'. So, the talk is about the next **learning** system rather than the next **education** system. Even the word 'system' is sometimes questioned on the grounds that it implies a degree of mechanical imposition. But if we actually, or mentally, prefix the word with flexible - a flexible learning system - it helps people see that what is being proposed is a not a free-for-all or laissez-faire.

A system can also be monitored, although the purpose of that monitoring will be to provide high quality advice and information, so that learners can make informed decisions and improve their performance, rather than the motive of the imposition of uniformity and standardisation.

The word and idea of standards chosen and imposed from above, can be replaced by the idea of profiles of personal achievement, an approach which has worked in other European countries, such as Denmark and Sweden, for decades. These can include generalised assessment tests by personal choice.

A recent MORI poll, commissioned by the *Campaign for Learning,* found that 90% of adults were favourably inclined towards further learning for themselves. In the right environment, they were willing to undertake further learning. The bad news is that 75% said they were unhappy and alienated in the school environment, and that, therefore, they preferred to learn at home, in the local library, at their workplace - *anywhere* other than a school-type setting. The old vocabulary and thinking just has to go, and not just in this country. As Edward de Bono says on his web-site:

"I have not done a full survey or review of education systems around the world so that the views I express are based on personal

experience. I would say that all education systems I've had contact with are a disgrace and a disaster."

My verdict is the same, though I find that some are more counter-productive than others. But, in the end, they are all deserts and we should not allow ourselves to be confused because we encounter the occasional oasis along the way.

3. The natural curriculum

A curriculum can be defined, in simple terms, as 'a course of study'. Knowledge can be taken, for now, to be 'some kind of content that is the substance of a curriculum'.

The latest research on the brain tells us that babies 'hit the ground running' as active learners. Their brains are already programmed to begin their lifelong course of study by interacting with their environment – unlike a cow, say, that is programmed to work in set routines. Indeed, one definition of what it is to be human is given in the title of a John Holt book – we are human because we are *Learning All the Time* (Ticknall: Education Now, 1991).

The 'natural' curriculum is the 'course of study' that humans develop as fast as physical and other conditions permit. So, babies accumulate knowledge through activities such as play, imitation, and interaction with any adults around. Play is best seen as children's work: one grandparent noted recently that her granddaughter, at the end of a refreshment and chat break, suddenly said, *"I must get on with my play-work now."*

The content of this natural curriculum is a set of existential questions. They include: Who am I? Who are you? Who are they? Where do we belong? Who gets what? How do we find out? Where are we going? How am I doing? Who decides what? It is a set of questions that stays with us permanently with the answers being reviewed constantly throughout our lives, as we assemble our tool-kit of knowledge. From time to time, we may engage with those attempts at systematic bodies of knowledge called subjects, to help provide some answers to some of these questions.

The question, 'Who am I?' will be redefined many times. As a person passes through the roles of infant, child, adolescent, young adult, single person, couple, married person, parent, older person, their self-concept has to be revised.

When young children reach five, they are asking, on average, 30 questions an hour based on their natural curriculum. At this stage, one provisional answer to the question of 'How do we find out?' has been gained, by achieving competence in the mother tongue.

Until quite recently in human history, this natural curriculum was sufficient to keep most of us going throughout life. But then, about 150 years ago, an institution called the compulsory school was introduced. And suddenly, the natural curriculum was displaced. The natural questions became replaced by an imposed curriculum based on THEIR questions, THEIR required answers, and THEIR required assessment. The message is dramatically changed: *"Your experience, your concerns, your hopes, your fears, your desires, your interests, they count for nothing. What counts is what **we** are interested in, what **we** care about, and what **we** have decided you are to learn."* John Holt, in *The Underachieving School*, p. 161 (Harmondsworth: Penguin, 1971).

In her study of children after one year of schooling, entitled *Rules Routines and Regimentation,* (Nottingham: Educational Heretics Press, 1996) Ann Sherman found that this message was already being absorbed, but with considerable reluctance. Children were aware of the 'hijacking' process, but felt powerless to do anything about it, and saw no alternative but to surrender to it. Ironically, this process is called giving young people their 'entitlement'. What is achieved by this substitution of a false entitlement in place of the real one? Richmal Crompton's William was puzzled: *"When I ask my father anythin' about lessons he always says he's forgotten 'cause it's so long since he was at school, and then he says I gotter work hard at school so's I'll know a lot when I'm grown up.*

Doesn't seem sense to me. Learnin' a lot of stuff ... jus' to forget it, ..."

In the textbook, *A Sociology of Educating*, (London: Continuum, 1997) I outlined three theories of knowledge. They were past-based, present-based and future-based. Subjects belong to the past-based category since they are relying on the arrangement of knowledge set up by our ancestors. They have **some** uses as part of the tool-kit of knowledge, but to overstress their importance is to indulge in a kind of ancestor-worship.

The world of subjects is fragmented, but the world and human experience are holistic. There are no boxes in the real world separating History from Geography or Mathematics from Science or Chemistry from Physics. There are no such things as Biology, or Economics or Sociology out there. But because the world and human experience are vast, we choose, for convenience, to look sometimes at one part of reality, and to ask certain kinds of question about it. We may be thinking like a historian; if we look at another part, ask another question, we may be thinking like a biologist, or an economist, or a psychologist, or a philosopher. But these different ways of looking at reality can trap us into serious distortions. Subjects can easily become a superstition and be held up as **the** tool-kit rather than a useful part of it.

Present-based knowledge is much closer to the natural curriculum idea and addresses current topics such as the mass media, terrorism, fashion, poverty – the agenda of newspapers and television investigations. All these require integrated forms of knowledge and draw on subject know-ledge only as appropriate.

Future-based knowledge is different again, and stresses the need to acquire the outlook and skills of the researcher. It starts with a realist appraisal of what we can know: *"We are all of us, no matter how hard we work, no matter how curious we are, condemned to grow relatively more ignorant every day we live, to know less and less of the sum of what is known ...I expect to live my entire life in uncertainty about as ignorant and uncertain and confused as I am now, and I have learned to live with this, not to worry about it. I have learned to swim in uncertainty the way a fish swims in water."* (John Holt, *The Underachieving School,* p.142 and p144 (Harmonsworth: Penguin, 1971)

It has become a commonplace to say that in the future, the key knowledge will be 'knowing how to learn' and also 'how to unlearn'. I think we can be more precise than this and say that the key knowledge, though not the only useful knowledge, is to be a **confident and competent researcher**. This requires knowing where information can be found, how to ask appropriate questions, how to check out good answers from bad answers, how to question the questions. The internet and computers can be valuable aids in this task of becoming a habitual researcher. Schools, with subject learning as their aim, are poor at this, since success in school has come to mean remembering the answers to teachers' questions long enough to repeat them in tests.

John Holt tells us how he answered one young learner's question about how to learn history: *"I said, "I think you may be asking me two questions: one, how do I learn more about history, and two, how do I get better grades in history class in school? The first thing to understand is that these are completely different and separate activities, having almost nothing to do with each other. If you want to learn more about how to find out about what things were like in the past, I can give you some hints about that. And if you want to find out how to get better grades in your History class, I can give you some hints about that. But they will not be the same hints."* (preface to *Learning All the Time,* Ticknall: Education Now, 1991)

When people say that we should learn and memorise things that may be useful to us in the future, we should remember that this is the **'squirrels and nuts'** theory of education. Squirrels collect nuts, bury them and then try to locate them later – a dubious idea on which to base a learning system.

George Bernard Shaw declared that *"What we want to see is the child in pursuit of knowledge, not knowledge in pursuit of the child."* I take this as a plea to return to the learner-managed 'natural' curriculum, with personal learning plans supported by adults providing a catalogue of learning possibilities. Our society has been information-rich for many years now, and we have even more possibilities than before through computer access to a kaleidoscope of web-sites. We have the technology and know-how, **we can rebuild the natural curriculum**.

* * * * *

Postscript: The story of the animals and the birds

The animals and birds decided to create a school. They devised subjects for study which were climbing, flying, running, swimming and digging. They could not agree on which was most important, so they said: *"Everyone must do everything – in case they need these things in the future".*

The rabbits were expert at running, but some nearly drowned in the swimming class. The experience shook their confidence and they could no longer run as well as before.

The eagles were terrific at flying, but very poor at digging and were assigned to extra digging classes. This took up more and more time, and some forgot how to fly well. And so on with the other animals and birds – moles became less confident at digging, otters at swimming.

The birds and animals no longer had the opportunity to shine in their best areas because they were all forced to do things that did not respect the natural curriculum.

The eagles got a bit fed-up with digging. They called a meeting of the birds to discuss the situation.
"We need a curriculum suited to us birds," they said. Everybody agreed.
"Nest building should be a core subject." All agreed.
The eagles spoke: *"The best nests, 'real' or 'proper' nests, are made of twigs on high ledges, because they are the nests of us eagles - the 'high flyers', as we say, with our 'high culture'."*
Now eagles are big and powerful and liable to eat smaller birds, so that was somewhat reluctantly agreed.

So kingfishers and wrens and lapwings and swallows all tried to build nests of twigs on high ledges. It was not easy when you were used to holes in river banks, or weaving cocoon-like structures of grass and moss, or plastering mud under the eaves of houses.

What was needed was a stage of lower ledges - a kind of 'key stage one' of nest building. *"It might help,"* the eagles said, *"if you wore our brown speckled uniform. Nobody seems to know why, but learning seems to go better if you wear a uniform. So, well done sparrows, you already have the right idea, but you kingfishers ... well, we love the gear, and all those nice bright colours ... but for learning, you will need to put on a brown speckled uniform."* And so the experiment continued in brown speckled uniforms.

But, the swallows went south for the winter. In the rest periods they talked about the new curriculum. Nests on ledges were rather draughty. The ledges had got rather crowded and some bullying incidents had taken place. What was wrong with mud-plastered nests on the side of warm buildings, anyway?

The swallows resolved to be brave and confront the authority of the eagles: *"When we get back we shall demand the right to have a diversity of nest types again."*
"Yes, and we shall demand the right to manage our own learning."
"And if we decide the best thing is learning in the family and not under the supervision of the eagles, we shall demand the right to resume the natural curriculum!"

Part two: Parents

1. Reluctant educational heretics

"There must be in the world many parents who, like the present author, have young children whom they are anxious to educate as well as possible, but reluctant to expose to the evils of existing educational institutions." This is Bertrand Russell writing in 1926 (*On Education*, London: Unwin) in the middle of the 'good old days' of 'traditional' schooling.

In 1977 a small group of 'educational heretics', who felt the same as Russell did in 1926, met in a farmhouse near Swindon. They set up a small co-operative that would provide mutual support to any attempts of its members at home-based education. It was to be known as *Education Otherwise*, the title being derived from the clause in the 1944 Education Act declaring that education was compulsory for children aged five upwards, either by attendance at school, **or otherwise**.

My wife and I were not able to attend the first meeting but joined in the next gathering in Worcestershire at the home of Iris and Geoff Harrison, Wanda, Andrea, Grant and Newell. Some group members, representing about ten families, had already started home-based education, others were considering doing so, yet others were concerned to give support to such an initiative.

The idea was not new since many famous, mostly creative people, such as Yehudi Menuhin, had been educated this way. What was new was extending the practice from the well-to-do, to 'ordinary' people. None of the early members of *Education Otherwise* had much in the way of material resources. Many today are still well down the social class pecking order and money-based wealth scales.

One task I undertook was to research this development. Twenty-five years later we have an extensive and international body of data about home-based education. The first finding is a negative one: there is no one right way. Actually, home-based educators rather take it for granted that there is no one right way of achieving effective learning and set about it in a variety of ways, child to child and family to family. They have, in the process, stumbled on the ideas of multiple intelligences, more than thirty different learning styles, the new research on the 'organic' brain characteristics, and the principles of accelerated learning, without necessarily being able to articulate them. The message is clear: it is a waste of time and resources trying to find the one right way of learning anything and our government is letting us down badly by pretending otherwise, with its dreary bullying apparatus of a National Curriculum, testing, league tables, and its oppressive inspection procedures

In 1997 I completed a book that celebrated the achievement of UK home-based educators, entitled *The Next Learning System: and why home-schoolers are trailblazers* (Nottingham: Educational Heretics Press, 1997). It has already been said that this book enables home-schoolers to hold their heads high, for most are reluctant educational heretics who, at first, are uncomfortable about their 'heresy' in questioning the dogmas of mass schooling. But it is **they** who are ahead - it is the others who are behind and risking their children in an obsolete schooling system:
"When my friends or neighbours tell me that I am so brave to take on home-based education, I contradict them. I say that they are the brave ones because they hand over their children to a bunch of complete strangers and then hope for the best."
(Bev. Turpin-West, Worcestershire home-educator).

The research questions have changed over the years. In 1977 the central question researchers in UK, USA and elsewhere were asking was, *"Can children educated at home match the performance of children at school?"* Were parents putting their children at a disadvantage with their home-based education programmes? If they were, it was implied, they might have to be over-ruled.

As the evidence came in, it became clear that children educated at home, performed much better than their school-based counterparts, being on average two years ahead on any aspect tested, and up to ten years ahead in above average cases. In areas not usually tested they were also ahead, such as personal confidence, self-esteem, oracy, deep learning, creativity and adaptability. They were ahead in social maturity, social skills and emotional maturity. This confounded those who did not understand that the social life of school, being of limited scope and range, was a drag on development.   It could hardly be otherwise, for 15,000 hours of enforced time in the company of people of the same age, and as immature and inexperienced as yourself, is not a good recipe for growing to maturity. Indeed, it impedes and distorts it:

"People can't understand when I say it's because of, not despite, my home education that I'm outgoing and able to cope with group situations. Having to learn to work by myself has also prepared me better for college, and university ..."

Kate Cardue, Coventry.

The more perceptive higher educational institutions recognise this. A letter from Boston University Undergraduates Admissions Director proclaims:

"Boston University welcomes applications from home-schooled students. We believe students educated primarily at home possess the passion for knowledge, the independence, and self-reliance that enable them to excel in our intellectually challenging programs of study."

Ironically, there was concern in one study by Jack A. Sande (*Home School Researcher* Vol 11, No. 3, 1995, p. 7) that showed that home-schooled children *were not as far ahead* in mathematics tests as they were in other tests:

"Most home-schoolers scored significantly higher than both their public school counterparts and national norms, but math scores showed the least advantage."

Now if we took research seriously, the implication of these findings would be that children should be discouraged from attending school, because they would be at an inevitable disadvantage - exactly the reverse of what had been feared!

Instead of such conclusions being drawn, however, the question began to change. It became: *"Why were home-schooled children so successful?"* The reasons form a complicated network, which is why I had to write a book to explain them. But here are a few clues. Home-based educators:

- create a learner-friendly learning environment. (Some schools try to do this, but few succeed. They create in John Holt's famous verdict, a prolonged course in 'practical slavery'.)
- are able to exploit our information-rich society at will. (Schools still rely on 'cultural mechanics' called teachers, to bolt on selected information and ideas.)
- use one of the most powerful methods of learning - structured conversation between two or up to eight people - at will. (At school this becomes replaced by one of the least effective methods of learning, i.e. crowd instruction, especially as the learners grow older.)
- build on the early successes of helping their children to learn to walk, their mother-tongue, and become competent in their home environment and neighbourhood, by continuing to use, and have confidence in, the principles of natural learning, as championed by John Holt in his ten books.
- discover the approach of the **catalogue curriculum** without necessarily knowing it or appreciating its total contrast with the totalitarian nature of an adult imposed compulsory curriculum such as a National Curriculum.

School is now the second-best option as well as being the most expensive. Home-based education has been shown in Australia to achieve superior results on less than half the pupil-cost of the average school. Choosing the 'best buy' of home-based education can, however, involve successes and strains, inspiration and grit, delights and despair, but as one parent declared:
"A bad day at home is a whole lot better than a bad day at school."

Although it is **possible** to educate badly at home, I have not yet witnessed any cases over the twenty years that I would regard as deficient. They have been good, very good or outstanding. There have been reports of religious recluse families in USA which have been a cause for concern. I have been told by officials of an occasional 'fake' home-educating family that is a cover for mere truancy. It may also be the case that unsuccessful families are likely to 'cease trading' fairly quickly and opt back into a school.

On the other hand, I observe that it is **possible** to achieve effective education of one kind or another in schools, but it is much rarer than you think, and mostly confined to a small number of democratic-tending schools, or particular classrooms with inspired teachers. So, there are oases in the desert, but **mostly it is desert.**

The research is now moving on to a third question. *"What can we learn from the reluctant heretics, to develop a better learning system suited to the needs of life in the 21st century?"* The answer is that home-schoolers are well ahead in developing and field-testing many of the features needed in the next learning system to replace our current obsolete one. We just have to learn some important lessons from their success. Canada has made a start: the province of Alberta has already set up ten cyber-schools linking home-based educators with each other, and with schools.

2. Parents as researchers

Twenty educationalists including home-based educators, head teachers, industrialists and researchers, met at the University of Nottingham in the Autumn of 1997. They spent two days exchanging ideas on the theme of education in the year 2020. One thing everybody agreed on straight away was that the climate of uncertainty, due to continuous change, would not go away. Continuous adaptation was here to stay.

In this situation, parents will have to become active members of the learning society themselves, and become constant researchers. By this, I do not mean writing research papers, but asking questions and sifting evidence and any offered answers. Tolstoy suggested that the only real objective of education was to **create the habit of continually asking questions**. (Governments are not always disposed to agree, finding passive minds more acceptable.)

There is another reason why parents need to become researchers. A few years ago, a student on a Master Degree in Education course became wearied by the constant procession of research studies presented week after week. He asked me to tell him what, in my opinion, all the studies told us in the end. I asked for time to think about it. Next week I gave a verdict. *"What they tell us,"* I declared, *"is that we do not know how to do it. We do not know how to educate children in a complex and changing world. If we knew, we would not have to research it any more. All the research is doing is trying to find useful clues."*

This statement still holds. But we do have more and better clues than before. But it means that parents do not have to believe over-confident teachers and educationalists, just as patients do not have to believe over-confident nurses and doctors. We can sift the evidence for ourselves, especially with the aid of magazines like *Natural Parent!*

Asking questions may lead to unexpected conclusions and actions. Those reluctant educational heretics, the home-schoolers, decided that they could make decisions based on their experience and the available evidence, that were at odds with 'professional' opinion. They may have even come to the same conclusion as George Bernard Shaw who proposed that *"all professions are conspiracies against the laity"*; well, some of the time anyway, if not most of the time in some cases.

One danger of parents thinking for themselves is that they may be regarded as eccentric. We can take comfort from the words of Bertrand Russell when he said that we should not fear to be eccentric in thought, because **every idea that is now taken for**

granted, was once said to be eccentric. It is not the case, however, that being unorthodox guarantees that you are right. There are many possibilities for error, and plenty of unorthodox ideas are dubious, or prove to be just plain wrong.

Becoming a researcher is a permanent state, because in the situation of continuous change, solutions are likely to be temporary expedients. The task might often be to decide the lesser of evils rather than achieve any certain answer. Or the task may be to replace familiar skills with new ones. The computer field illustrates this well. When I wrote a book with my Amstrad 8256, I thought learning all the new skills was well worthwhile. Before long I needed to learn again to work with a PC and Word for Windows. Now I am learning yet again to take on the new skills needed for my voice-driven computer.

One shortcut for parents to become well-briefed in educational ideas is to be found in the use of quotations. For example, when Mark Twain said that he *"never allowed schooling to interfere with his education"*, he drew attention to a number of propositions. One is that schooling and education are not the same thing, and can often be entirely opposed. Another is that your own private investigations, conducted in your own time and in your own way, can be valid education. Indeed, one of the reasons why schooling and education can be in opposition is that the questions and concerns of the learner can gradually become replaced by the official questions and concerns imposed by others and, even more oppressive, the officially approved answers.

For a second example, take the quotation from George Bernard Shaw when he says: *"What we want to see is the child in pursuit of knowledge, not knowledge in pursuit of the child."* This quotation alerts us to a fundamental objection to a national curriculum or any adult imposed curriculum. It turns learning into a 'child-hunt' where knowledge hounds the child rather than a 'knowledge-hunt' where learners are encouraged, supported and advised in their seeking out of knowledge. Because I found quotations to be such a powerful aid to thinking, I compiled a book of quotations on education. People tell me it is useful to stimulate discussion, question assumptions, and expose myths and superstitions.

Another shortcut is the use of analogies. When people say that we should learn and memorise things which may be useful to us in the future, we can try to think of other examples of when things are done now in the hope that they may be useful later. The activity of squirrels comes to mind. They collect nuts, bury them and then try to locate them later. Are we being asked to believe that children should collect adult-designated nuts of information, then bury them in their memory, in the hope that they may need to dig them out later? Is this the most effective way to spend time?

For another analogy, Edward Fiske, former New York Times Education Editor, concluded that getting more learning out of our present schooling system was *"like trying to get the Pony Express to beat the telegraph by breeding faster ponies."* An analogy like this alerts us to the ancient nature of mass schooling and its growing obsolescence due to slowness to adapt. Perhaps tinkering with the system is like getting the stagecoach to go faster by strapping roller skates on the hooves of the horses, when what is needed is a new kind of transport altogether, such as a railroad.

It helps to locate useful sources of information, but I think it was Winston Churchill who said it is better to read wisely than widely. You could read every newspaper every day, but I doubt if it would be worth the effort, and it is better to choose one that does not insult your intelligence. *Natural Parent* is one useful source, and *ACE Bulletin* from the Advisory Centre for Education, set up to advise parents, is another. I think *Education Now News and Review* is also good, but I must declare a vested interest here.

Finally, the title of 'parents as researchers' is, perhaps, misleading. It might well read 'families as researchers' since adults and children alike will need this mentality to cope with our ever-changing world and our own slow-to-adapt schooling system. In addition, **purposive conversation** among family members and others, about these and any other matters, is one of the most effective methods of learning we know.

- The address for the Advisory Centre for Education is Unit 1B, Aberdeen Studios, 22 Highbury Grove, London N5 2EA (Tel: 0207 354 8318)

3. Purposive conversation and effective learning

We live in an age of continuous change and the constant revision of knowledge. So, I proposed earlier that we parents need to become constant researchers. This means noting any useful ideas in new books. Here are three that challenge, inform and develop new interpretations about education. On the face of it, they are about 'full-time' home-based education, but they all ask fundamental questions about education in general. And since we are all 'part-time' home-based educators in the large gaps around school hours, they apply to us all.

The most recent one is *Educating Children at Home* by Alan Thomas, (London: Cassell, 1998), a psychologist interested in individualised learning methods. Since schools have a poor track record in individualisation, he turned to home educating families in both Australia and the UK, where individualised learning is 'business as usual'. But what impressed Thomas was the amount that occurred largely through social conversation with an adult. He noted a remarkable amount of spontaneous incidental talk. Personally, I prefer to call this **purposive conversation** to distinguish it from ordinary social exchanges. Thomas reminds us of the research that shows that high achieving 'genius' children have a background of both individualised attention and purposive conversational learning, which are found to be major factors in their accelerated intellectual development.

The research of Alan Thomas is based on a hundred home educating families. He shows that at home, lessons are concentrated and intensive. Little time is spent on the distractions that absorb so much time in classrooms.   With increased efficiency, lessons are short and often confined to the mornings only, and this leaves plenty of time for extra purposive conversation.   Not all families use formal lessons.   So, in their case, even more time can be given over to purposive conversation.

Next, learning at home becomes an interactive process rather than a series of tasks to be tackled.   Therefore, any mistakes that are made, rather than creating barriers to learning, becomes steps on the route to enlightenment.   In this interaction, concepts are acquired, skills improved and new knowledge is gained during the course of concrete, everyday activities or through topics that have captured the learner's interests.   Parents and children can be unaware of the efficiency and power of their learning regime. Parents remarked that it was only when they looked back over a period of time, or kept a careful record, that they could see just how much high-quality learning had taken place.

Thomas reports that, *"The initial worries which home educators have concerning social development gradually fade as they see their children growing up, confident and relaxed in adult company and able to relate to children of all ages."*   Parents come to see that it is actually the school that is cut off from the real world.
The research concludes that home educators give us a view of education, which, in many respects, is markedly different from what is on offer in school.   Their approach has the potential to bring about the most fundamental change in education since the advent of universal schooling in 19th-century.   But we will need a new kind of institution in place of schools to bring this about.

The second book is *Strengths of Their Own: home schoolers across America* by Brian D. Ray (Salem: N.H.E.R.I publications, 1997).   In a mere 139 pages packed with information and analysis, Dr. Brian Ray, director of the USA National Home Education Research Institute, presents the results of his recent study of home-based education.   He took a USA nation-wide sample of 1657 families and their 5402 children, and all 50 states were represented.

The results support his earlier findings that indicate that home-based education is the best option available, and that schooling, whether private or state, is now the second best choice. Michael Farris, of the Home School Legal Defence Association, is quoted as saying that:

"... parents who take personal responsibility for the education and socialisation of their children reap a harvest of exceptional children who are well prepared to lead this country into the next century."

The growth of home-based education in the USA seems unstoppable. At first, it was estimated that the numbers would flatten out at one percent of the school-age population. Now that it has forced its way past five percent in various States, some think it may peak at 10%. But good news is infectious, and others now predict that 50% of all children within a generation, will be learning in home-based education, some full-time and some for 50 % of their school-age time, in flexi-time arrangements.

The research identifies the positive outcomes of home-based education on topics as varied as students' academic achievement, social and psychological development, and the performance of the home-educated when they become adults. Adults who were home-educated are, typically, in employment rather than unemployed, independent-minded and entrepreneurial in outlook, and think positively about their previous home education experiences.

The study explodes the 'lack of socialisation' myth. Children were engaged in a wide variety of social activities spending, on average, 10 hours a week in such things as music classes, play activities outside the home, sporting activities, church organised groups, Scouts and Guides.

In an earlier study, 58 percent of families have computers in the home. In Ray's latest study, this has risen to 86 percent. The children use computers for educational purposes, but the only subject to which there was a significant positive difference, was reading, since those using computers scored higher in reading tests.

A personalised, self-designed curriculum was used for 71 per cent of the students, rather than a set, purchased package. The programme selected a variety of elements from the information-rich society in which we now live, including some pre-packaged items. Ray, like Thomas, explores the methods of learning and also identifies purposive conversation, as a key reason for the success of home-based education.

Ray suggests that home-based education may eliminate, or at least reduce, the potential negative effects of certain background factors. He shows that the success of the home educated is unrelated to low family incomes, low parental educational achievement, parents not having formal training as teachers, race or ethnicity of the student, gender of the student, not having a computer in the home, starting formal education late in life, or being in a large family. He explodes the myth that home-based education is for the well-off, since the average family earnings for home-educating families was below the national average.

Finally, there is the intriguing indication that **'the family that learns together, stays together'**; home-educating families show signs of being more stable, with their members more fulfilled and happy as a result.

The third book is *The Art of Education: reclaiming your family, community and self*, by Linda Dobson, (Tonasket: Home Education Press, 1995). For Linda Dobson, school erases key abilities such as curiosity, imagination, creativity, inner peace, humour, artistry, self-motivation, and intuition. In return, school offers *'indoctrination in accepted ideas'*.

School develops bad habits, Dobson observes, and a notable one is learning to rely on experts to solve problems for us. For Dobson, home-based education is **family-centred education** where the members grow into self-reliance and healthy scepticism of experts and professionals. It uses the principles of natural education which require only a guide to provide encouragement, support, some direction, and a learner ready to discover and create goals and values that are personally meaningful. In appendix A to the book, the list of famous adults who were home-schooled includes seven presidents of the United States and various scientists, inventors, authors, explorers and business people.

In proposing that the government way is an inadequate one, and that family-centred education is superior, Dobson sets about exploding various myths about home-based education. She does this by describing a day in the life of a home educator. All the wealth of learning she lists, are *"accomplished in the warm, loving, safe environment of home! No bells, no tests, no peer pressure, no competition! Individual attention, individual progress, individual choice! The art of education - pure, stressless, naturally occurring."*

We learn how the Dobson family began home-based education. The oldest child's brief stint in public school kindergarten had already revealed a number of worrying features. There was the stress of formal book learning begun too soon. Then there was the behaviour-altering effects of peer pressure. Next, there was the personality-altering effects of school discipline. Finally, there was the dispiriting effects of boredom and irrelevance.

Home-based education worked for the children, but also expanded the life of Linda Dobson:
"As the children acquired basic skills - reading, writing, arithmetic - their interests expanded. So did mine. Their sense of wonder blossomed. So did mine. Their abilities multiplied. So did mine. Their confidence increased. So did mine."

Some friends were impressed but protested that they could not cope with being with their children all day long. They failed to see that the irritating behaviour of their children is a consequence of schooling. Other friends worried about the cost, but the sum of money needed is flexible, especially now that we live in an information-rich society with plenty of free resources available.

Another gain was a strengthened family life:
"Our institutions still give lip-service to the family as the first and most important building block society. But by destroying the

natural cycle of love and respect, inherent in family life through their demands that children 'socialise' in artificially created institutional settings, they are contributing to the destruction of society itself."

Human beings, she declares, are capable of wise decision-making when they are not paralysed by authoritarian hierarchies or impersonal structures that diffuse individual responsibility.

The radical thought is developed that education could be improved with one simple reform - **eliminate schools**. Instead, establish learning centres dedicated to meeting the unique needs of all the learners who took up the invitation to attend. Several examples of these learning centres are described: Paris, Lexington Virginia, Providence Rhode Island, and Kansas City, and the *Centre for Personalised Education Trust* is supporting the founding of such centres in UK.

There is a fourth book, also by Linda Dobson, which is of particular interest to anyone actually starting or considering full-time home-based education. It is *The Home Schooling Book of Answers: the 88 most important questions answered by home schooling's most respected voices* (Rocklin: Prima, 1998). All the books listed above are obtainable from HERO Books, 58 Portland Road, Hove, East Sussex BN3 5DL Telephone 01273 775560]

4. Damage limitation

Every parent is a home-based educator until children reach the age of 5.   After that, all parents are still home-based educators, although some are full-time, whereas others use schools for part of the time, during the weekdays, on those weeks the schools are open. For those who either choose to use schools, or necessity forces them to, I want to open up the question of damage limitation.

I had to face this question when, some years ago now, my son reached the age of five. His mother, Shirley, was an experienced infants teacher, and I was an experienced secondary teacher and teacher educator. With our insider knowledge, we both understood the serious limitations of compulsory mass schooling, whether state or private, and set out to offer him a home-based education alternative. Ironically, he elected to try school, so his parents had to turn their attention to mounting a damage limitation programme. Why was this necessary?

A few years ago I wrote an article entitled *"Schooling can seriously damage your education"*. I now think I was too cautious and should have entitled it, *"Schooling **will** damage your education"*. The only question in my mind is how much damage will be done and in which dimensions.
There is **some** good news about schooling, however, as Everett Reimer (*School is Dead*, Harmonsworth: Penguin 1971) indicated when he wrote,
*"Some true educational experiences are bound to occur in schools. They occur, however, **despite** school and not because of it."*

Some teachers manage, despite our domination-riddled schooling system, to swim against the tide of restrictions and regulations, and create episodes of genuine humanity and genuine learning. I tried to be such a teacher and so did my wife Shirley. As my son put it, the good news was that he was able to find *"bits of treasure in the wreck"* of the schooling system, because of such teachers.

It is also true that the homes of some children are despotic or neglectful, so that even a coercive school provides a respite. Schools also provide a respite for parents from their children, so that they can pursue their careers, golf, or whatever.

But the long-term effect of mass, compulsory coercive schooling is damage. As the New York prize-winning teacher, John Gatto put it, he was employed to teach bad habits. These ranged from bad intellectual habits, bad social habits, bad emotional habits, to bad moral and political habits. Neither the 'successful' pupils nor the 'unsuccessful' pupils escaped. For starters, he identified seven of these bad habits. (*Dumbing Us Down: The Hidden Curriculum of*

Compulsory Schooling, Philadelphia, New Society, 1992)

John Taylor Gatto recognised that what he was really paid to teach was an unwritten curriculum made up of seven ideas. The first was **confusion.** He was required to teach disconnected facts, not meaning, infinite fragmentation, not cohesion. The second basic idea was **class position.** Children were to be taught to know their place by being forced into the rigged competition of schooling. A third lesson was that of **indifference.** He saw he was paid to teach children not to care too much about anything. The lesson of bells is that no work is worth finishing: students never have a complete experience for it is all on the instalment plan.

The fourth lesson was that of **emotional dependency** for, by marks and grades, ticks and stars, smiles and frowns, he was required to teach children to surrender their wills to authority. The next idea to be passed on was that of **intellectual dependency.** They must learn that good people wait for an expert to tell them what to do and believe. The sixth idea is that of **provisional self-esteem**. Self-respect is determined by what others say about you in reports and grades; you are *told* what you are worth and self-evaluation is ignored. The final, seventh lesson is that **you cannot hide**. You are watched constantly and privacy is frowned upon.

The consequence of teaching the seven lessons is a growing indifference to the adult world, to the future, to most things except the diversion of toys, computer games, 'getting stoned' as the height of having a good time, and violence.   School, Gatto concludes, is a twelve-year jail sentence where bad habits are the only curriculum truly learned. School 'schools' very well but this is not education. Paul Goodman went further when he entitled his book *Compulsory Mis-education,* Harmondsworth: Penguin, 1971.) The system mis-educates, he argued.

But all this is good preparation for being gullible to the other controlling institutions, especially television.   This is a theme developed in Gatto's book (op.cit).

In contrast, home-based education can be seen as analogous to organic farming – a system with the toxins avoided. Our 'damage limitation', however, meant 'building up the immune system' to fight the toxins of the schooling system.

Other parents were puzzled. Why did we see what they saw as 'good' schools, which today would get OFSTED approval, as *'educational impoverishment zones'*. *'A good uniform means a good school'*, they declared. *'And probably a bad education based on mindless uniformity'*, we responded.
John Gatto had an explanation for this puzzled response by others:
"It is the great triumph of compulsory government monopoly mass-schooling that ... only a small number can imagine a different way to do things."

So what did our policy of damage limitation look like? The first item was a principle: we would never pretend the school was right when it was wrong. If it proved necessary and with our son's approval, we would take the trouble to challenge the school when it was in the wrong, even if this meant we were labelled 'nuisance', 'interfering', or 'bad' parents. Part of this principle was never to shirk a dialogue with our son about what was happening in school and its implications. Thus, when a teacher, unable to find a guilty party, punished the whole class, we pointed out that this was a common fascist procedure, but also why the authoritarian system pushed teachers into this corner.

The second item was a positive programme of activities to offset some of the bad habits John Gatto identified. To some extent, we just continued the programme of activities used between the ages of zero and five years, providing a learner-friendly environment that was personalised and democratic, stressing fun and happiness. This involved construction toys, board games, electronic games, watching TV programmes together, playing games in the garden or park - business as usual in fact.

We located out-of-school clubs and activities such as Judo groups, holiday soccer coaching courses, holiday table tennis events, and provided transport for groups of friends to go skating in the evening. One 'bit of treasure in the wreck' was the Local

Education Authority's Saturday morning orchestra facility. This encouraged young musicians to gain experience with their own or with loaned instruments, in beginner ensembles and, eventually, to the senior orchestra. The Local Education Authority also had an Outdoor Centre in Wales and an Arts Residential Centre which were sources of worthwhile week-long courses.

The local naturalist society had regular Sunday outings to gardens, arboretums, bird watching sites ranging from woodland to moorland, to seashore - even to sewage farms where we could view birds such as black terns – all in the company of enthusiasts. On occasion, we found ourselves at the Gibraltar Point Field Station for a weekend of investigation, where father gained 'brownie points' for being the first to notice a rare red-backed shrike. The *I Spy* booklets were a useful cheap resource but another favourite purchase was the magazine, *The Puzzler*.

We organised our own day trips to seaside, to parks with fun-fairs, to houses, to cities and museums, to sporting events ranging from the local soccer and cricket teams to the world table tennis championships. There were National Car Shows and the Birmingham Show to experience. We involved ourselves in a local amateur dramatic society that welcomed children to help out backstage. Also, the family, including grandparents, would often come along to meet the families, when I was researching home-based education. There were package holidays abroad, to Sweden to visit friends and also to Spain.

Perhaps none of this seems all that remarkable, and families across the social range do some selection of these things, according to their means and inclinations. But we consciously and deliberately saw all these activities as opportunities for purposive conversation and mutual learning and an antidote to the effects of schooling. We could try to provide holistic and integrated learning to offset the fragmented approach of the school, and use any opportunities to practice the democratic skills of negotiation, consultation, agreement, accommodation and co-operation - the skills that auth-oritarian schools usually discount and discourage.

What was achieved?   Well, perhaps partial success could be claimed. Just choosing to be there, transformed the experience. At seven years, our son was telling us that, *'school did not get to him like the others, because he had an escape tunnel ready and waiting'*.

At eleven, he went to the Open Day at the secondary school where 300 children from the feeder schools in the district were in attendance, but he was conscious of being the only one making a decision whether to go or not. The others were conscripts. Later, we saw the head teacher where my son informed him that he was giving the school a term's contract to see how things went. I came to realise that my son regarded the school in the same way that an anthropologist regards a tribe being studied – he was in the role of a participant observer.

The switch from school to further education college was eventually a considerable release from the domination of schooling, and independence of spirit and mind were better able to flourish. On the other hand, moving away to university meant that this institution just had a field day. The intellectual dependence Gatto talks about now asserted itself in the form of courses and modules requiring replication of approved material and rejecting any alternative or independent analysis as a threat to the authority of 'experts'. (During twenty years working in universities, this is what I observed happening as a matter of course, and pointing it out in committees was never well received!)

Is a damage limitation policy really necessary? And does every parent using schools need one?   John Stuart Mill in *On Liberty* (1859, p177) observed that:

"A general State Education is a mere contrivance for moulding people to be exactly like one another, and as the mould in which it casts them is that which pleases the dominant power in the government, whether this be a monarchy, an aristocracy, or a majority of the existing generation ... it establishes a despotism over the mind, leading by a natural tendency to one over the body."

This seems to me to be just the opposite of an 'organic, toxin-free learning' outcome.

5. Grandparent power?

The phone rang. It was a grandparent. The voice said that the family had been talking about the possibility of home-based education. Children, parents and grandparents alike, were unhappy about the domination-riddled and learner-hostile schooling that they were experiencing. The parents were both out at work. What did I think about the grandparents undertaking to supervise home-based education? I replied that I thought that this was an idea well worth exploring.

There has been a trickle of inquiries from grandparents asking similar questions over the last twelve months. Since this has not happened in the previous 23 years that I have been researching home-based education, I am beginning to wonder if this is could be the 'start of something big', as the song title puts it. Is it the beginnings of grandparent power?

A recent report from Japan about classroom breakdown, contained the following paragraph. *"Classroom breakdown is a serious concern not just for the educators but for the business leaders who exercise influence in Japanese society. It was reported that in seminars targeted at business people ordinarily interested in little beyond matters of the economy, lectures on 'classroom collapse' drew noticeably larger crowds than usual. Their anxiety about what is happening to their young grandchildren, rather than their grown-up children, is notable."*

In the USA, public opinion on home-based education has shifted. The shift amongst grandparents has been a particular feature. In the book by Brian Ray, *Strengths of Their Own*, he reports that currently, 67 percent of grandparents supported the practice of home-based education in the family. About 22 percent were neutral, and only 11 percent were opposed. There has been a change here that follows the general trend, which is that in 1985, 73 percent of a Gallup Poll survey of the general population in USA said home-based education was a bad thing. In 1997 this had fallen to just over 50 percent. The reason suggested was that favourable stories about home-based education were in contrast with continuous nightmare stories about mass compulsory schooling. Interest has increased to the point that the Internet bookseller, Amazon USA, now lists over 200 books on home-based education, and they are selling steadily.

Demography also suggests the possibility of grandparent power. In UK, in 1901, life expectancy for women was 45 and for men it was 49. In 2001 life expectancy for women is expected to be 80 and 75 for men. By 2020, it is expected that 40 percent of the population will be over 50. All this amounts to a rapidly growing population of grandparents, and indeed, of great grandparents.

I recently saw a notice about a pack for grandparents which contained suggestions of ways in which grandparents can use books and stories with their grandchildren. It had been put together by the public library service, spotting the potential of grandparents. It had information about choosing books, helping children learn to write, do craft, do cookery, make puppets and telling stories. It was useful to grandparents whether their grandchildren were attending school or being home-educated.

A recent public opinion poll (MORI), commissioned in UK by the *Campaign for Learning,* found that 90% of adults, including plenty of grandparents, were favourably inclined towards further learning for themselves. In the right environment, they were willing to undertake further learning. The bad news is that 75% said they had been unhappy and alienated in the school environment, and that, therefore, they preferred to learn at home, in the local library, at their workplace - *anywhere* other than a school-type setting. More and more adults are uneasy at putting children through the same kind of schooling experience, now extended to 16,000 hours – double what some grandparents will have endured.

A recent newspaper article was entitled 'rise of the silver surfer'.

It showed how in the USA the over 55 age group has been the fastest-growing sector of American Internet users. The report showed how there was a similar trend to be found in the UK. It is also the case that computers are helping to break down the ageism of our social structure. The idea that the young cannot teach the old anything, is shown to be nonsense when you observe five-year-olds teaching their grandparents how to surf the Internet. Similarly, the idea that you cannot 'teach an old dog new tricks' is exploded by the 'silver surfers' phenomena.

Many of the ageist assumptions about learning have been exploded by the experience of the Open University. The idea that you cannot learn in old age is shown to be dubious when people are graduating in their 70s and 80s. As further evidence, John Holt wrote a book entitled *Never Too Late,* describing how he learnt to play the cello in his 50s. He reached performance level with the Boston Symphony Orchestra, thus refuting the idea that if you failed to learn a string instrument early, it became impossible later.

A USA grandparent, a former head teacher, recently wrote to me from California about the experience of his grandson:
"… we should start a campaign to 'scrap schools'. There is no hope to change them. I am working now with one small elementary where my grandson attends. It is a lousy school as you and I view learning – but sadly, it is better than most in the area. In trying to work with 20 teachers to find four who might start a non-graded, individualised school-within-a-school, I have yet to find one I would hire – let alone put in a new environment. They have no vision of what it could be – and are so overwhelmed by their daily personal lives, and the oppressive mandates of the district, that they have no chance to 'renew'."

None of the grandparents who have telephoned - often resulting in very long phone calls - have blamed individual teachers. It is the learning system of coercive, compulsory schooling that appalls them. *"My grand-daughter never did anything mean, underhand or spiteful until she went to school and began to learn some bad habits,"* said one. *"I have watched my lively, cheerful, bright grandchildren gradually losing their sparkle,"* said another.

They recognise a crucial fact about learning systems, that **how** you learn is as important, if not more important, than **what** you learn. Thus if you learn literacy in an oppressive regime, you become literate with the attitudes of oppression included. If you learn to read and write in a regime of co-operation and power-sharing, (such as Summerhill School), you become literate with democratic habits of mind. If you become literate in a flexible, learner-friendly home-based education regime, you become flexible, creative, resourceful and ... literate.

Many of the observations of the grandparents reflect the findings of the study by Ann Sherman, reported in her book *Rules, Routines and Regimentation* (Nottingham: Educational Heretics Press, 1996). She informally interviewed children in five different Midlands schools after they had had one year of schooling. Children felt that they were on the receiving end of a crushing process that they endured with considerable reluctance. Children were aware of a 'hijacking' process, where their interests, feelings and concerns were disregarded, but they felt powerless to do anything about it, and saw no alternative but to surrender to it. Ironically, this process is described as giving young people their 'entitlement', when, in truth, it can be seen as taking some of their humanity away.

Some grandparents are starting to find their voices and speak out against 'the deadening of the spirit of their grand-children'. They want a celebration of the joy of learning, sometimes recognising that the primary school classrooms their own children experienced had visitors from all over because they were, at least, pointing in a more humane direction. If this protest continues to increase, long live grandparent power!

Part three: learners and learning systems

1. Order! Order!
Three kinds of discipline and four kinds of error

When my son was four-years old, he told me off me for kicking our plastic ball on to a rosebush. We were playing football at the time. He was quite right because we had agreed the rule that this was not the thing to do, since it could puncture the thin skin of the ball. I accepted his reprimand. Quietly, I did claim extenuating circumstances - that it had been accidental and not a deliberate act. My father, who witnessed the incident, was horrified. Later he accused me of corrupting the child by weakening my authority as an adult. He was one of those people who think that discipline is the simple problem of adults making children behave to instructions.

This is only one kind of discipline - the authoritarian. Three kinds can be identified. They are:
1. **Authoritarian** - where order is based on rules imposed by adults. Power resides in an individual or group of leaders. Its slogan is: *"You will do it my (or the management's) way!"*
2. **Autonomous** - where order is based on self-discipline and self-imposed rational rules. Power resides with the individual. Its slogan is *"I did it my way."*
3. **Democratic** - where order is based on rules agreed after rational discussion, i.e. based on evidence, human rights values and the logic of consequences. Power is shared amongst the people in the situation. Its slogan is, *"We did it our way."*

There has been a centuries-old debate about which of these three is the best system of discipline. It is now a sterile debate. The complexities of modern life are such that **all three types of discipline** have a part to play in the scheme of things. Sometimes we need to follow instructions, or take on leadership roles, thus following the authoritarian approach. Therefore, in an aeroplane, debating who should fly the aircraft and the rules of flying is not the appropriate form of discipline that matches the situation. In a car, however, drivers need autonomous discipline and to make the decisions about driving the car without the confusions of being over-ruled by an authoritarian or advised by a committee of back-seat drivers.

In many other situations, such as running a 'convivial' rather than a 'coercive' school, many heads are likely to be better than one, in deciding the rules to be adopted, based on the evidence and the rights of all involved. This is democratic power-sharing, and although it can be time-consuming at first, it leads to better, fairer, and accepted decisions with a co-operative system of order.

There are three types of error as regards the question of discipline. One, the current error of most UK schooling, is to select the authoritarian as the exclusive or predominant approach. The second, the error of some radical thinkers, is to make the autonomous the One Right Way. The third error, from another radical tradition, is to make the democratic the exclusive approach. All these One Right Way approaches fail to match the need for young people to learn what most of their elders have clearly failed to learn, that is, how to be competent in the logistics and practice of all three types of discipline, and to select them appropriately.

A fourth error is to regard all three as of equal status and allocate equal time to them. In the modern world, the democratic form of discipline is, in the end, the most significant, firstly, on the grounds that Winston Churchill proposed - that democracy is the worst form of organisation - **except for all the alternatives.** It follows, that if you do not have democratic discipline controlling the others, you will inevitably have something worse such as tyranny, domination, bureaucracy, or bullying authoritarianism.
The democratic form of discipline has another feature that marks it out as the framework into which the others slot. It can incorporate the other two. To illustrate this point, when I trained teachers using the 'heretical' democratic approach, where the group planned, administered and evaluated their own programme of

learning, with the services and support of the paid tutors acting as learning coaches, the group would delegate considerable amounts of the preparatory work to be done autonomously by individuals. In deciding the best way to learn a particular theme or skill, the group would sometimes choose to submit to an authoritarian form of learning as appropriate for that particular task.

Teachers have proved that the democratic approach is effective with all ages of children. Head teacher Bernard Trafford in his book *Participation, Power-sharing and School Improvement*, (Nottingham, Educational Heretics Press, 1997), shows how this is working in Wolverhampton Grammar School. John Ingram and Norman Worrall, in their *Teacher-Child Partnership: The Negotiated Classroom*, (London: Fulton, 1993), show how this works with infant and junior classes. Families, whether home-schooling or not, who discuss, negotiate, and share decision-making, also engage in democratic discipline.

In contrast, the One Right Way approaches have a strong tendency to 'play cuckoo' and heave the eggs of the others out of the nest. The error of some radical educators was to allow no place at all for the authoritarian approach. Apart from the need for 'discipline flexibility' in the modern world, authoritarian control is sometimes necessary to protect children, but always, as Bertrand Russell proposed, **in the spirit of freedom**. This means that it is a temporary expedient only, until one of the other forms of discipline can take over. Explaining the reasons to children is then essential as a prelude to agreeing rules and reasons. 'For your own good' and 'because I say so', the stock in trade assertions of so many authoritarians, are not good enough reasons in themselves.

The sad conclusion is that most schools in the UK, by ignoring the democratic form of discipline, are doing their pupils a grave disservice. The result, Chris Shute argues in his book, *Compulsory Schooling Disease*, (Nottingham: Educational Heretics Press, 1993), is that the obsessive use of authoritarian imposed discipline is the actual cause of many of the social problems it sets out to 'cure'. Such schools are involved, as they have been since the start of compulsory schooling, in compulsory mis-education.

2. Where does the bully mentality come from?

The problem with most discussions about bullying is that it is concerned with the immediate 'first aid' problem of how to deal with the latest outbreak of persecution. There are now plenty of books, booklets and articles that try to deal with this, (see Kidscape details that follow), so I intend to look beyond the symptoms to the causes of the disease.

The root causes of bullying are usually overlooked or passed off as some weakness of character. Alice Miller, in her work, however, proposes that people **learn** the bully mentality. She concludes from her research that 'every persecutor was once a victim'. She shows how every member of the Third Reich had the same kind of upbringing and education based on unrelieved domination, and she calls this 'the poisonous pedagogy'.

But, I want to come closer to home than Hitler's regime. School in UK, based on the current model of the compulsory day-confinement centre, is itself **a bully institution.** In a democracy, nobody is supposed to be detained against their will unless they have committed an offence. So, what is the offence that children have committed to justify detention? It would appear to be that their 'offence' is that they are young.

Having confined children by compulsion, apart from those who opt for home-based education, schools employ **a bully curriculum** - a compulsory National Curriculum or some other imposed programme. We could employ a democratic curriculum if we wanted to, and the catalogue curriculum, which offers a more-or-less unlimited range of learning possibilities and is learner-driven, is just such an approach.

Just how ingrained is the idea of adults imposing their ideas of 'proper' learning is indicated when a school does it differently. Sudbury Valley High School in USA has no timetable and no lessons until the learners request them or set about organising them. It operates a learner-driven curriculum.

The bully curriculum is enforced by the increasingly favoured **bully pedagogy** of teacher-dominated formal teaching.   Alice Miller's view that this is a 'poisonous pedagogy' is supported by others.   Rosalind Miles entitled her book, *The Children We Deserve,* (London: Harper Collins, 1995).   Paul Goodman chose the title of, *Compulsory Mis-education* (Harmondsworth: Penguin 1971) and Chris Shute used the idea of, *Compulsory Schooling Disease* (op.cit).

In another book, *Dumbing Us Down: The Hidden Curriculum of Compulsory Schooling*, (Philadelphia: New Society, 1992) John Gatto Taylor, has the following to say:
"I began to realise that the bells and the confinement, the crazy sequences, the age segregation, the lack of privacy, the constant surveillance, and all the rest of the national curriculum of schooling were designed exactly as if someone had set out to prevent children from learning how to think and act, to coax them into addiction and dependent behaviour."

He decided to change his style of teaching, to give children space, time and respect and to see what happened. What happened was that the children learnt so much that he was nominated teacher of the year for the New York State, several times.
Gatto recognised that what he was really paid to teach was a hidden or unwritten curriculum. He decided it was made up of seven basic ideas. I have mentioned these before, but I think they are worth repeating. The first was *confusion.* He was required to teach disconnected facts not meaning, infinite fragmentation not cohesion, and a tool kit of superficial jargon rather than genuine understandings.   The second basic idea was *class position.* Children were to be taught to know their place by being forced into the rigged competition of schooling. A third lesson was that of

indifference. He saw he was paid to teach children not to care too much about anything.

The fourth lesson was that of *emotional dependency* for, by marks and grades, ticks and stars, smiles and frowns, he was required to teach children to surrender their wills to authority. The next idea to be passed on was that of *intellectual dependency*. They must learn that good people wait for an expert to tell them what to do and believe. The sixth idea follows on from this - the teaching of *provisional self-esteem*. Self-respect is determined by what others say about you in reports and grades. People learn to be told what they are worth and self-evaluation is ignored. The final, seventh lesson, is that *you cannot hide*. You are watched constantly by teachers, parents and other students and privacy is frowned upon.

Responses to his analysis are predictable, Gatto says, the assertion that there is 'no other way': *"It is the great triumph of compulsory government monopoly mass-schooling that among even the best of my fellow teachers, and among even the best of my students' parents, only a small number can imagine a different way to do things."*

School, Gatto concludes, is a twelve year jail sentence where **bad habits** are the only curriculum truly learned. School 'schools' very well but it hardly educates at all. All this schooling, however, is good preparation for being gullible to the other institutions that control us, e.g. television.

Currently the school system in UK is reinforced by the bully compulsory assessment system and an aggressive school inspectorate. The unwritten, but powerful message of this package, is **adults get their way by bullying.**

There are at least three types of outcome to this model of schooling. The 'successful' pupils grow up to be officially sanctioned bullies in dominant authority positions as assertive politicians, doctors, teachers, civil servants, journalists and the like, and start their own career as persecutors.

Next, a majority of the 'less successful' learn to accept the mentality of the bullied - the submissive and dependent mind-set. Such people need someone to tell them what to think and do, because they have been prevented from learning how to do 'joined-up' thinking.

A third outcome is the production of a group of free-lance bullies who become troublesome and end up in trouble of varying degree of seriousness. Until we replace this domination model with a different model, the root causes of bullying will continue. As Jerry Mintz reports from the USA:

"American kids like watching violence on TV and in the movies because violence is being done to them, both at school and at home. It builds up a tremendous amount of anger... The problem is not violence on TV. That's a symptom... The real problem is the violence of anti-life, unaffectionate, and punitive homes, and disempowering, deadening compulsory schooling, all presented with an uncomprehending smile."

We can do better than schooling based on domination and I applaud the work of those teachers like John Gatto Taylor who begin to move away from domination towards participation, power-sharing and democratic relationships (see also Trafford below). They organise schools councils that work. They have parental involvement that is genuine. They devise lesson and classrooms based on co-operative principles. They make it possible for children, in the words of my son, *"to find bits of treasure in the wreck."* But, knowing it is a wreck is crucial to positive survival in it.

As one young person said after reading a book of educational quotations, (*The Freethinker's Guide to the Educational Universe*, Nottingham: Educational Heretics Press, 1994) *"Now I know that there are other people who think school is crackers, I can cope with it."*

* * * * *

- Parents faced with problems of bullying at school can find help in: *Preventing Bullying: A Parent's Guide* by Kidscape. Send large SAE for a free copy from Kidscape, 152 Buckingham Palace Road, London SW1W 9TR

• Bernard Trafford's book is, *Participation, Power-sharing and School Improvement* and costs £9-95 (p.&p.included) from Educational Heretics Press, 113 Arundel Drive, Bramcote Hills, Nottingham NG9 3FQ

3. Back to the future?

Headline: Chief Inspector of Schools Condemns National Curriculum!

"I am ashamed to have been a party to it," he says.

Teaching has become a debased activity according to the Chief Inspector of Schools:
"In nine schools out of ten, on nine days out of ten, in nine lessons out of ten, the teacher is engaged in laying thin films of information on the surface of the child's mind and then after a brief interval he is skimming these off in order to satisfy himself that they have been duly laid".

These observations of the Chief Inspector of Schools, made in the early 1900s, can hardly fail to sound a controversial note in the UK today. At present, it is hard for anyone to suggest that there may be more to education than a ceaseless quest for a better way to force-feed information to children.

But the man who was responsible for supervising the first National Curriculum of the early 1900s, was the Senior Chief Inspector, Edmond Holmes. He wrote a report in which he condemned all that he had been doing for the last thirty years, and admitted his sense of shame for being a part of it. He had to resign as a result of telling the truth as he saw it. He went on to write two books establishing his case, but his inconvenient views were quietly buried. *"He appears in histories of education as a footnote, or as one whose ideas are acknowledged but never allowed into the main current of thinking, either in his own time or later,"* writes Chris Shute in his recent book, *Edmond Holmes and the Tragedy of Education,* (Nottingham: Educational Heretics Press, 1998).

If England wanted to have an education system fit for a new century, Holmes declared, it would have to stop telling children what to do and compelling them to do it, since this produced only passivity, lassitude, unhealthy docility or, in the stronger, more determined spirits, 'naughtiness'. Uniformity was just plain bad education. Holmes wrote of the *"... tendency (of the examination system) to arrest growth, to deaden life, to paralyse the higher faculties ... to involve education in an atmosphere of unreality and self-deception."* He called this system a source of *'infinite mischief'* which obscured the true purposes of education.

One of the most disturbing features of the current educational scene is that we have now entered the new century with exactly the same basic model of mass, uniform, conscription-based schooling that Holmes saw as a tragedy. The battery-hen, 'tell them then test them' approach still reigns supreme. Holmes was a committed Christian and saw all this as unchristian; if God had intended us for uniformity, we would have been created so, as in the case of ants or bees. Therefore he saw the imposition of a uniform curriculum on children by adults as an affront to his religion.

Holmes was not the only whistle-blower. Bertrand Russell declared that there must be in the world many parents, like himself, who had young children they were anxious to educate as well as possible, but reluctant to expose to the dulling effects of 'tell them and test them' schools.

Next, Albert Einstein observed that:

"It is in fact nothing short of a miracle that the modern methods of instruction have not entirely strangled the holy curiosity of inquiry; for this delicate little plant, aside from stimulation, stands mainly in need of freedom; without this it goes to wrack and ruin without fail."

Another whistle-blower, Winston Churchill had this to say on the matter:

"Schools have not necessarily much to do with education ... they are mainly institutions of control where certain basic habits must be instilled in the young. Education is quite different and has little place in school."

Education officials responsible for the drafting of 1988 Education Reform Act, which re-established the 1904 form of curriculum, also wanted 'institutions of control' for they were recorded as saying:

"We are in a considerable period of social change. There may be social unrest, but we can cope with the Toxteths. But if we have a highly educated and idle population we may possibly anticipate more serious social conflict. People must be educated once more to know their place."

Are there any current glimmers of hope? Well there are several. The first and most radical is the home-schooling movement which, based on the growth rate of the last 20 years, is now expected to account for 25% of the USA school-age population by the year 2008. UK appears to be running about five years behind.

The second is flexi-time. By 2008 there may be a further 25% of USA children on flexi-time arrangements - 65,000 families are reported as taking up the options of ISPs (Independent Study Programmes) this year, in California alone. UK authorities are resistant on this one and tend to oppose flexi-time arrangements if requested by parents but, hypocritically, use them if it suits their own purposes.

Thirdly, the Charter Schools movement has been growing apace in USA in the last five years, based on the Danish and Dutch models. Here groups of parents, sometimes in co-operatives with teachers, set up small schools or local learning centres with State aid.

Fourthly, most USA States have made a start in replacing schools with All Year Round Education Centres which open eight in the morning until eight at night, every day of the year. These centres are able to offer much more flexibility in learning opportunities to fit the needs of individuals, families and adult learners and much more flexible contracts for teachers. These institutions are also in a position to offer Independent Study Programmes.

A catalyst in these developments can be, and often is, information and communications technology, (ICT), which enables the development of cyber schools, learning networks, virtual schools and other flexible, computer-linked possibilities. ICT also allows initiatives with truants. In Japan, teachers communicate with truants using e-mail and multimedia technology, sometimes holding video conferences with the children. The feedback has so far been positive. Michael Fitzpatrick, in *Times Educational Supplement,* 10/4/98 reports that the approach stems from the view that bullying and the pressure to succeed are driving pupils to truancy and sometimes suicide.

Another glimmer of hope is contained in the words of Prime Minister Tony Blair: *"... the revolution in business ... will, over time, take place in education, too. We will move away from a system that assumes every child of a particular age moves at the same pace in every subject, and develop a system directed to the particular talents and interests of every pupil."*
These words carry a serious implication. If he can envisage a better system of learning, what are we waiting for? Are the present generation of young learners being fobbed off with a second-rate experience for no good reason? Why is he tolerant of the current schooling system devoted to the regressive ideology of education based on fear and domination, that Holmes despised?

What can parents do about all this? Our local councillors, national politicians and journalists need to be educated about these things. Letters to newspapers asking questions about these matters, even when they are not published, help influence opinion and so do letters to MPs. Introducing these ideas into conversations also helps. The growth of home-based education, for example, has taken place mostly by word of mouth and through a trickle of newspaper and magazine articles. Why not ask your MP about the words of Tony Blair and their implications? I would be interested to have copies of any replies.

The anthropologist Margaret Mead encourages us: *"Never doubt that a small group of thoughtful, committed people can change the world. Indeed, it is the only thing that ever has."*

* * * * *

Edmond Holmes and 'The Tragedy of Education' by Chris Shute, ISBN 1-900219-12-3, published by Educational Heretics Press, costs £7-95, from 113 Arundel Drive, Bramcote Hills, Nottingham NG9 3FQ

4. It's not what you learn, but the way that you learn it ...

As a young teacher, interested in improving the learning methods at my disposal, I came across this learning league table from National Training Laboratories, Bethel, Main USA. It ranked a number of learning systems on the basis of how much the learners remembered.

	Average retention rate
Formal teaching	5%
Reading	10%
Audio-visual	20%
Demonstration	30%
Discussion Group	50%
Practice by doing	75%
Teaching others	90%
Immediate use of learning	90%

There is, of course, much more to learning than memorising facts, (although this has a part to play in the scheme of things) and these include the questions of which system motivates learners best, and which produces deep learning rather than shallow learning.

I simply refused to believe the evidence about retention rates, however, and threw myself into a whole host of strategies to prove the figures wrong. The pre and post-test results I recorded showed again and again that the research was correct.

Yet the learning system still in most common use in schools and universities is formal crowd instruction. Enthusiasts for the crowd-instructor role tend to ignore the evidence about its levels of efficiency. The short-term recall of learners after formal instruction averages 10% with a usual range of 0% to 20%. The long term recall averages 5% with a usual range of 0% to 10 %. This is why so much homework and revision work is needed to shore up the inefficiency of the learning method.

All this information helped set in motion a life-long interest in learning systems and led to me write a textbook, *A Sociology of Educating*, (London: Continuum, third edition 1997). But it might easily have been entitled 'The Study of Learning Systems'.

A first finding is that there exists a considerable variety of learning systems and each one produces different results. Bertrand Russell, in *On Education* (p.28, London: Unwin 1926), states the consequence like this: *"We must have some concept of the kind of person we wish to produce before we can have any definite opinion as to the education which we consider best."*

So, first decide your intentions, then choose an appropriate learning system. Thus, if we accept the view that the world's most pressing need is to produce **people who will do no harm**, to the environment, to each other or to themselves, and maybe even do a little good, then learning based on co-operation has to replace that based on competition.

I will illustrate something of the variety of learning systems from my own experience, firstly, from teacher training. When I began work in teacher training I was required to use formal, instructional methods. These were the same methods that had been used on me when I trained to be a teacher, and the intention was to introduce two basic roles. The first was that of **crowd-control steward,** since a great deal of time is spent dealing with large groups of conscripted learners. Conscripted learners, like conscripted slaves, are not likely to be automatically pleased about their enforced activity, especially as they grow older, and therefore need marshalling. The other basic role was that of **crowd-instructor**.

There was some general dissatisfaction with this crowd instruction model at the time I moved from classrooms to begin teacher training in 1970. This led to some ideas in UK that schools should encourage a bit more participation, and even try more democratic modes of learning. I offered trainee teachers the chance to work in a different learning system, that of a democratic learning co-operative, (DLC). They could plan the course, learn and teach it in ways they determined, and review progress as they went along. I would switch my role from *'the sage on the stage'* to the *'guide on the side'*. For fifteen years, 1972-88, trainee teachers had this choice and each year, rather bravely I thought, opted for the DLC system. I was joined in this work by Clive Harber, who was later recruited by the University of Natal to help develop the new South African democratisation of schools policy, which was started under the Nelson Mandela government.

The contrast between the type of teachers produced under these two methods was dramatic. Some comments from the end-of-course evaluations written by the students using democratic methods are indicative:

"For the first time I became responsible for my own education which stimulated motivation and a desire to learn. Lack of motivation at school and even at university had been the main reason why I had not enjoyed study. I can honestly say that I have actually enjoyed attending seminars for the first time in my academic life ..."

"There was intellectual enjoyment. Intellectual explor-ation became an exciting and satisfying end in its own right, rather than as a means to a boring and worthless end ..."

"The co-operative spent many hours in discussion and formulated opinions and views (often varying) in relation to our timetable of work. All the group members felt, without any reservation whatsoever, that the co-op was a new working experience which was stimulating, enjoyable and very worthwhile."

I was startled, but delighted, to find a considerable leap in standards when I used this approach in teacher education courses. So were the external examiners and inspectors who, never having encountered this approach, knew nothing of its theory or practice. As well as being more successful in the standard tasks of memorising and reproducing institutionally approved material, the students also increased standards in other respects. These included resourcefulness, flexibility, curiosity, skills in co-operative learning, readiness to unlearn, research techniques, enhanced personal confidence and strong feelings of community and mutual support amongst the members of the learning co-operative.

Another illustration from my own experience is the contrast between school-based learning and home-based learning. The new initiatives in home-based education in UK began in 1977, so I began to research them, since they presented a holistic learning regime of a quite different kind from mass schooling. Until then, home-based education had been an option for rich families, with the most well-known case celebrated in the popular film, *The Sound Of Music* cataloguing the experiences of the Von Trapp family. But now, home-based education began to be implemented by 'ordinary' families right across the social scale.

I found contrasts. Learners from home-based education usually achieved superior results in academic achievements, emotional intelligence, and social maturity. In addition, there were bonus skills of resourcefulness, flexibility, curiosity, skills in co-operative learning, readiness to unlearn, research techniques, enhanced personal confidence and strong feelings of community amongst the members of the family. Interestingly, the results of the learning co-operatives and home-based education showed many similarities.

My own interest was stimulated by the experience of taking my student teachers into schools in the morning, and finding the creation of a lively interest in learning rather like toiling uphill, with the wind and rain in my face. We had some successes, but it was hard-going.

In the afternoon, however, I could find myself working with a family or group of families with children of the same age as in the morning. But now it felt like striding downhill with the breeze on my back and the sun shining. It suddenly seemed to be easy-going creating a lively interest in learning. Over the years, I teased out the reasons for this contrast and set some of the results down in a book, *The Next Learning System: and why home-schoolers are trailblazers,* (Nottingham: Educational Heretics Press, 1997).

How do you classify learning systems in a way that will show that the way you learn is a critical issue? None of the attempts I looked at seemed to be getting us very far. Here is the approach I developed which classified systems as Authoritarian, Autonomous and Democratic, along with a fourth category of Interactive:

The Authoritarian View of Education or, *"You will do it our way".*
In **authoritarian education**, one person, or a small group of people, makes and implements the decisions about what to learn, when to learn, how to learn, how to assess learning and the learning environment. This often decided before the learners are recruited as individuals or meet as a group. As an exclusive method, it is favoured by totalitarian regimes because it aims to produce the conformist, lockstep mentality.

The Autonomous View of Education or, *"I did it my way".*
Here, the decisions about learning are made by the individual learners. Each one manages and takes responsibility for his or her learning programmes. Individuals may seek advice or look for ideas about what to learn and how to learn it by research or by consulting others. They do not have to re-invent the culture, but interact with it. As an exclusive method it is favoured by liberal or libertarian regimes.

The Democratic View of Education, or *"We did it our way".*
In **democratic education**, the learners as a group have the power
to make most, or even all, of the key decisions, since power is
shared and not appropriated in advance by a minority of one or
more. Democratic countries might be expected to favour this
approach, but such educational practices are rare and often meet
with sustained, hostile and irrational opposition.

The Interactive View of Education, or *"We did it in a variety of
ways".*
Here, the authoritarian, democratic and autonomous approaches
are used in a variety of patterns. They may be alternated, or
revolved or used in some order of ranking. Thus in the last case of
ranking, a learning co-operative may work with democratic
methods as the major approach, but use autonomous methods when
individuals are delegated to prepare learning experiences for the
group, or authoritarian methods when the group decides this is
appropriate for a particular task.

This classification helps demonstrate a key lesson from the study
of learning systems - that HOW you learn is as important, if not
more important than WHAT you learn. It is not just what you
learn, but also the way that you learn it

As an example, let us take literacy. It assumed that literacy is
automatically a good thing. But, learning literacy in a bully
institution makes you a literate bully. Richard J. Prystowsky, in,
Paths of Learning, Autumn 1999, reminds us that at the Wannsee
conference, January 20th 1942, high-ranking Nazis met to plan the
'Final Solution to the Jewish Question'; that is, for the destruction
of European Jewry. Over half of the conference participants had
PhDs – a cohort of highly literate bullies.

When someone proposes that literacy is the aim of the learning
system, we need to ask, "what kind of literacy?" Are we to
produce literate fascists, or literate totalitarians? Do we want
literate democrats, or a literate minority composed of the greedy

and super greedy? If we want literate male chauvinists, we need single sex institutions.

The attitudes and habits of mind absorbed along with a learning system have been referred to as the 'hidden curriculum'. More accurately, since they are not all that hidden, it is the 'unwritten curriculum'.

As governments world-wide bang the drum for more education, Don Glines of *Educational Futures Projects*, USA, introduces a sobering thought:

"... the majority of the dilemmas facing society have been perpetrated by the best traditional college graduates: environmental pollution; political ethics; have/have not gap; under-employment - (in fact) the sixty four micro-problems which equal our one micro-problem!"

If some of the highly literate are responsible for many of the major problems that now face the world, perhaps we need less 'education' and more 'wisdom'?

If you want to produce people with democratic habits, discipline and understanding, or self-directing and self-managing people, then you will need to adopt a learning system that will do this. Thus, a current mistake in UK is the citizenship initiative, believing that **preaching** the virtues of democracy from within an authoritarian learning system will do the trick. It fails to work, and can be counter-productive in producing cynicism. South Africa, in adopting various measures to democratise its schools, has displayed much more wisdom.

The US radical, Nat Needle writes a protest in response to President Clinton's call to US citizens to learn to be super-competitive in what he predicted will be the most ruthless century yet:

"... if the 21st century becomes the story of human beings around the world pitted against each other in a struggle for well-being, even survival, this will only be because we failed to imagine something better and insist on it for ourselves and our children.

"I don't care to motivate my children by telling them that they will have to be strong to survive the ruthless competition. I'd rather tell them that the world needs their wisdom, their talents, and their kindness, so much so that the possibilities for a life of service are without limits of any kind. I'd like to share with them the open secret that this is the path to receiving what one needs in a lifetime, and to becoming strong."   (AERO-Gramme, No. 25, Fall 1998)

But, you can learn the habits and attitudes Needle prefers only if you establish an appropriate learning system. We are a long way away from having such a system.

5. Beans in a jar and the domination of the peer group

Here is a simple demonstration of the power of the peer group. A class of young people, or a similar gathering who know each other, is asked to inspect a jar of beans, in turn and without discussion. After examining it, they are asked to pass the jar on and to write down on a piece of paper their estimate of the number of beans in the container. The demonstrator collects the pieces of paper as the estimates are made and keeps them in order.

In the next stage, the jar of beans is circulated again, and the class or group is told that it can revise its estimates. This time the estimates are called out in turn, to the class or group. As each estimate is called out the demonstrator logs it on a flipchart or blackboard. It becomes plain that after the first two or three calls, other members of the group start to revise their original estimates so that it is close to the standard or norm that they see emerging. Individuals may make quite big revisions to make sure they are close to the group norm. Gradually, the group norm appears on the chart.

The demonstrator can now plot the original estimates on the chart and start a discussion as to why the patterns are not the same.

Individuals may explain that when they heard the estimates of other members, they felt the need to revise their own estimate. Some may explain that when two or three seem to agree, they thought that they must be right, and that they lost confidence in their own estimate.

The group norm that emerges maybe far removed from the true number of beans in the jar. And individuals who revised their estimate to be close to the norm, can have been right all along. There may be a few independent individuals who stick to their own personal estimate against the group norm, but these are usually rare. Such individuals can also be more accurate than the group norm. But they can be subjected to banter and derision or worse, for sticking to their judgement.

This demonstration is based on some classic experiments on factors affecting group judgement, conducted in the 1930s by Jenness, and written up in the psychological journals of the time. I have used the beans in a jar event many times in the past to start discussions on the influence of the peer group.

All this pressure to abandon your own judgement and conform to the group norm is generated merely over estimating the number of beans in a jar. When more serious matters are at stake, the pressure increases. *"... if you don't wear Nike trainers and Addidas top and trousers, you are the laughing-stock of the school. I don't know who starts these trends, but they mean everyone needs a computer, a mobile phone, 'in' clothes ... to be cool."* Catriona McPhee, aged 12, in, *Living Green* 32, Summer 2000.

'Once in school, they'll learn to hate each other.' This was the title of a newspaper report by David Hill about a new book entitled *Prejudice*, by Cedric Cullingford.   The report, in *Guardian Education*, 3/10/00, proposed that in theory, prejudice has no place in the classroom, but in practice, that is precisely where it breeds.

Once the habit of dividing people into 'one of us' or 'not one of us' is established, it continues in other contexts. Recent research carried out at Lancaster University on football supporters found that they failed consistently to come to the aid of an injured supporter from a rival team.   Secret cameras filmed an actor apparently writhing in pain on the floor.   When the actor wore a Manchester United shirt, 80 percent of Manchester fans came to his aid.   But when he wore a Liverpool shirt, all but a handful walked straight past.

'They used to want a revolution.   Now they just want money,' was the title of an article *in The Observer* November 11th, 2000.   It quoted surveys commissioned for *The Observer* demonstrating that any teenage tendency of the past to rebel against the system, had given way to the current peer group identification with consumerism.   *"I love labels.   If it doesn't have the label, I won't buy it.   Labels are everything.   It's about looking right, being part of something, of a group,"* said one.   The survey showed that for 14 to 16 year-olds, friends are twice as important as family.   Four out of five rate 'having a good time' and music as 'most important to me'.   Designer clothes are more important than the environment and making money rates higher than helping others, the survey showed.

In *Natural Parent*, November/December 1998, I noted some other examples of negative socialisation:

Report 1: Children now expect bullying to be a regular feature of school life.   This was the conclusion of a national survey commissioned by the *Family Circle* magazine showing that eight out of ten have suffered at least once sustained attack.   On average, the first bullying experience can now be expected at the age of eight.

Report 2: A report commissioned by the Suzy Lamplugh Trust showed that weapons are now carried by one in ten school students.   Although this is much lower than the USA, the trend is upwards.   Indeed, a later study published in the British Medical Journal in April 2000, reported that around a third of 11 to 16 year-old boys and 8 percent of girls in Scotland, had carried weapons ranging from knives to replica pistols and knuckledusters.   The study showed that those who were involved in drugs, were more likely to carry weapons.

Report 3: Primary Schools are to be issued drug guidelines by the Head Teachers Association, (HTA). Solvent-sniffing is now found to be common among children as young as 7. The HTA claimed that schools were choosing to sweep the problem under the carpet by not informing the police, in order to protect the reputation of the school. The primary school peer group is now a child's key source of information about drugs. As the youngsters grow older, their peer group will supply information about smoking, alcohol, ecstasy tablets, and expensive teenage fashion. A government survey on drugs, published in November, confirmed a rising trend in the use of drugs amongst schoolchildren. By sixteen, 39% had tried drugs, 55% cigarettes and 73% alcoholic drinks.

John Holt put the peer group agenda in perspective when he wrote: *"To learn to know oneself, and to find a life worth living and work worth doing, is problem and challenge enough, without having to waste time on the fake and unworthy challenges of school - pleasing the teacher, staying out of trouble, fitting in with the gang, being popular, doing what everyone else does."* (*Teach Your Own* Liss: Lighthouse 1981, p.64 -5)

All this helps explain why one reason for starting to educate children at home is to replace the predominantly negative socialisation of school, with the predominantly positive socialisation of a home-based education programme, operating out-and-about in the community. One home-educating parent, as noted earlier, made the comment, *"People often say to me, 'You are so brave'. But I reply, 'No, you other brave one, because you hand your children over to a bunch of strangers, and hope for the best'."* She might have added, *"And you hand your children over to the domination of the peer group, and hope for the best"*.

Ironically, the domination of the peer group is brought into being by the adults who created an ageist institution called school in the first place, and those who continue, foolishly, to perpetuate its existence. The idea that press-ganging all young people of the same age, and more importantly, of similar immaturity, into one place for a total of at least 16,000 hours, year in, year out, will somehow lead to emotional and social maturity, is dubious, if not absurd. It plainly does no such thing. The next learning system has to deconstruct the ageism of the present one and create all-age, community, invitational learning centres. (It is feasible, however, to have some age-grouping within a non-ageist institution for particular purposes and as a temporary phase or expedient - such as early childhood groups.)

We do not have to look far to see how such institutions they can work – the public library is just such an institution, and so is the family. I have often answered the question of what do we do with the current schooling system by suggesting we close it down completely. Then we hand the plant and personnel over to the library service asking it to expand its educational brief beyond books, and multi-media information materials to the organisation of invitational community learning centres with courses, classes and group activities such as orchestras and drama. The public library has many of the features required in the next learning system – it is non-ageist, it is invitational and personalised not coercive and standardised, and it also operates with a catalogue curriculum approach rather than a restrictive imposed curriculum.

What can parents who still have to use the flawed institutions of the schooling system do in the meantime? It is not going to be easy. The social psychological research on the difficulties of changing attitudes once they are established, is not encouraging. On the other hand, after one 'beans in a jar' event, young people were known to label as 'beanies' people who abandoned their own judgements merely to please the group, rather than discussing them. Thus the peer group had moved towards two key ideas in democracy – toleration of a variety of points of view and a need to explore these.

Therefore, constantly presenting the facts, such as the findings of the surveys given above, can be a start. Then there are some ideas in part two, section four of this book on damage limitation. At least it makes you feel better by at least doing something.

6. Instead of fear

For the last quarter of a century, the discussion of education and educational policy in the UK has used the language of fear, almost exclusively. Here are some of the pronouncements made by politicians, inspectors and civil servants that I have noted.

1. **"Fear is a great motivator"**
This statement was made in response to a question asking whether the speaker was conscious of the amount of fear implicit in OFSTED inspections based on the authoritarian ideology of education, the national curriculum, the national testing system, the invention and imposition of the stifling key stages and the school league tables. His response was *"Fear is a great motivator"*.

Without doubt, fear can be used in some situations, e.g. to make nervous human beings into soldiers ready to kill on command. But its place in creating confident, capable and inquiring learners is, to say the least, dubious. In his famous book, *How Children Fail*, (Harmondsworth: Penguin, 1969), John Holt demonstrated that fear-based strategies in the classroom were much more likely to have a serious long-term inhibiting effect: *"... they drive them into defensive strategies of learning that choke off their intellectual powers and make real learning all but impossible."*

2. **"There is to be no hiding place"**
This slogan has been used a number of times recently to indicate that people who question the official dogmas or do not conform unhesitatingly to orders from London, will be 'hunted down'. The people in question range from head teachers who make any kind of protest, to classroom teachers who protest about regimentation, to children who react badly to domination, to parents who question the wisdom of the system. More and more letters written on education to national newspapers claim the anonymity of 'name and address supplied' to avoid retribution.

3. **"Might is right"** and the **"leaders know best"**

This idea has been hailed as the mark of strong leadership. Some head teachers who have been held up in public meetings as models to be emulated, are those who go into so-called failing schools and impose their will on the teachers and the children. One observer wondered if he was the only one in the audience who thought the model he was being asked to admire, was that of the officially licensed bully. The consequence is that the bully mentality is legitimised and children absorb the message that, 'adults get their way by bullying' and may act on it then, or later.

4. "It is for their own good"
This pronouncement has been made several times to indicate that adults must be in charge and make children learn whatever the adults deem to be 'necessary learning'. The idea that children should have any say in the process, has been put down with the assertion that all this domination and imposition is 'for their own good'. Children gradually get the message:
*"Your experience, your concern, your hopes, your fears, your desires, your interests, they count for nothing. What counts is what **we** are interested in, what **we** care about, and what **we** have decided you are to learn." (p. 161, The Underachieving School,* Harmondsworth: Penguin, 1971)

5. "We need to employ 'tough love'"
'Tough love' has been used regularly to justify various aggressive and bullying approaches to educational problems. These range from smacking children to using the police force to round up truants.

Those born before 1950 will recognise these five assertions as popular with the leaders of the Third Reich. 'Tough love' was used as a justification for members of the Hitler Youth reporting any non-conformist tendencies or conversations that were witnessed at home. Parents or siblings would then be questioned and the necessary punishment meted out. Hitler Youth members were not to feel bad about reporting their parents - they would be only guilty of 'tough love'. It was, after all, 'for their parents and siblings own good'. 'Fear, being a great motivator' would cause people to behave in the required fashion, in time. 'There must be no hiding place', because, 'the leaders know best'.

If you consider that this thinking is peculiar to other cultures, watch this space! A committee considering the merits of re-instating National Military Service in the UK in the mid 1990s came out against the idea, but declared that another idea, that of a compulsory national uniformed youth organisation, had many merits, but that the time was not yet right.

Am I alone in thinking that a learning system based on and justified by coercion, backed by fear, insults the intelligence of teachers, parents and children alike? In what is supposed to be a democracy based on co-operation, the use of consent, and choice-respecting whilst being characterised by what Nelson Mandela saw as the **absence of domination**, why do we tolerate a totalitarian-style domination-riddled system of learning heavily rooted in fear? John Holt saw it as the enemy within: *"Meanwhile, education - compulsory schooling, compulsory learning - is a tyranny and a crime against the human mind and spirit. Let all those escape it who can, any way they can."* (Instead of Education, Harmondsworth: Penguin, 1977, p. 226)

Fear, of course, takes many forms. Schools are usually not granted the power of life and death over children. Only fairly recently, schools in the UK were denied the power of physical pain when corporal punishment was disallowed. A successful lawsuit in the European Court of Human Rights gave damages to a family objecting to their children being beaten. Fearing a flood of successful lawsuits, the government hurriedly change the law – one of those occasions when fear seemed to work.

Schools, however, retain the power to cause emotional, mental and psychological pain. Because they are places of coercion and not invitation, they can threaten, frighten, humiliate and denigrate at will, practising the arts of regressive education. Even 'progressive education' turned out to be a method of gently manipulating children rather than supporting their growth as autonomous beings. If you do not choose to be there, the result is, *"that for all the children some of the time, and for some of the children all of the time, the classroom resembles a cage from which there is no escape."* (Philip Jackson in *Life in Classrooms,* Eastbourne, Holt, Rhinehart and Winston, 1968)

Earlier, I explained that the fear of the peer group was a potent force for conformity. By clinging to the outdated idea of organising ageist learning institutions, we provide an ideal arena in which the peer group can operate its fear-based mechanisms with maximum, and often devastating effect.

Here are some alternatives to the use of fear, that are available to parents and to those in educational settings:

1. Invitation

Many of our public institutions use invitation instead of coercion. Shops invite you to purchase their goods. Public houses invite you to drink and eat. Travel agents provide a choice of holidays. Public libraries invite you to borrow books. Schools could also be places of invitation, although education could still be an expectation and a culturally sanctioned imperative.

But politicians, police and others, ironically, 'fear' the consequences - believing that children would not find the facilities on offer appealing – a devastating indictment in itself. According to opinion surveys, their fears are somewhat groundless, for over 95 percent of young people said they would still attend school if it was voluntary but noted that this alone would begin to transform their attitudes to the place.

2. Encouragement

One of the findings of recent brain research is that the brain chemistry changes under the influence of encouragement. A positive and receptive mind-set is created. But dis-couragement creates the opposite effect, and a defensive and avoidance mind-set develops.

3. Teaching by request

John Holt suggested that a principle of good education is 'no question, no teaching'. Until somebody has asked a question, nobody should be teaching anything. This hard dictum can be softened somewhat by including teaching by permission. An adults who asks, 'would you like me to try to explain ...' is respecting the learner's right to say, 'not just now, thank you'.

4. Dialogue

Dialogue is another non-hierarchical, non-coercive and respect-laden activity that can start in many ways. A simple, *"What do you think about this, Mary?"* is often enough to start a dialogue. Open-ended questions are more likely to stimulate dialogue than closed-end ones. There is not much scope in questions like, *"Did you get wet walking home in the rain?"*

5. Being an example

People who are making things, doing things, playing instruments, reading, or holding a discussion are all providing examples that may tempt the curiosity of others. If, in addition, they are prepared to answer questions or invite interested people to join in, dialogue and shared activity can result.

6. Seeking permission to be helpful

'Do you mind if I make a suggestion?' or 'Can I help?' are quite different in quality from, 'Step aside, I will take over now'. These interventions indicate some of the differences in attitudes between co-operation and domination. Seeking permission to be helpful is respectful of the other person, whereas asserted intervention is not.

7. Showing some trust in the learners

John Holt tells the story of a child who declared an interest in penguins. Recognising a 'teaching opportunity', he found a book on the subject and handed it over. Later he noticed that the book had been set aside. *"But I thought you were interested in penguins?"* he said. The youngster replied, *"Yes, but that book told me more about penguins than I wanted to know just now."* John trusted the child and accepted the verdict.

He could, of course, have opted for domination: 'You will never learnt unless you persevere,' or 'You should not give up with a book just because it is becoming complicated', or, 'Bring it here and I will go through it with you'. But he did not. Perhaps he remembered his own observation about young learners: *"They are afraid, above all else, of disappointing or displeasing the many anxious adults around them, whose limitless hopes and expectations for them, hang over their heads like a cloud."* (*How Children Fail*, Harmondsworth: Penguin 1969, p.151)

None of this should be news to parents. Most parents, as well as those teachers who strive to defeat the logic of the system, use the above strategies some of the time, and some use them most of the time. Parents use them when dealing with very young children when they are learning to walk, talk, and develop competence in their home environment. All the home-based educating families I have worked with use these strategies, almost without deviation. It is also the way we usually deal with our friends and acquaintances. What makes us think that respect, sensitivity and courtesy could ever be optional in the case of children?

Part four: teachers

1. What is a good teacher?

People are often shocked to find that there is no agreement about 'good' teaching. One view stresses that a good teacher is in the business of making themselves redundant. The American educator, John Holt, put it like this:
"A good teacher teaches you how to teach yourself better."
So the task of the teacher is to make themselves unnecessary as soon as possible.

Another view stresses the teacher as instructor, taking decisive action by using crowd control skills to organise learners. Then, using crowd instruction methods, the teacher tries to get the learners to memorise a particular piece of information or achieve a required understanding. This tends to be the officially approved view of 'good' teaching, that underpins the whole imposed apparatus of the National Curriculum, the Testing System and the OFSTED inspection ideology.

The third view sees the good teacher as supporting the growth of learning groups who direct and manage their own learning:
"Of a good teacher, they say, when the task is done, we did this ourselves!"
Actually, in saying this, the ancient Chinese philosopher Lao-tse, was proposing the characteristics of good **leaders,** but I suggest it applies to this particular view of teaching too.

There is a further definition of a good teacher - one who stimulates another person's researches. But, most of the 'my best teacher' articles that I have read, actually use the second model of 'teacher instructing me'. I must confess that I find these kind of articles rather repetitive and tedious. In contrast to this constant admiration for the instructor-teacher, my own 'best' teacher hardly spoke to me directly, apart from the usual pleasantries of 'hello', 'good-bye', and 'how are you?' He was the Co-operative Society Insurance Agent. He made our house his last call on a Saturday, since he knew that he would be certain to get a cup of coffee and a lively discussion with my father. I learned to make it my business to be in the room, reading or working, to listen in on these conversations, because new and exciting ideas were constantly being introduced. Charlie would mention a book, *The Ragged Trousered Philanthropist* by somebody called Robert Tressell. I would go to the library and investigate. Next time, he might mention a radical theologian named Peter Abelard, which meant another trip to the library. On another occasion he would quote a guy called Bertrand Russell, so that meant another search along the bookshelves. A person named Tom Paine apparently wrote an interesting book called *The Rights of Man,* so that needed checking out. On the subject of ghosts, he talked about the research activity of the ghost-busting British Psychic Research Association. I needed the assistance of the librarian to track this one down.

Charlie was a self-educated man, a W.E.A. attender I would guess, and had no formal qualifications to my knowledge, but I think he was the best educated person I ever met. He exemplified the character in Wesker's play, *Roots,* who declared that *"Education is asking questions all the time"*. Yet he seemed entirely content with his work in the Co-operative Movement. None of the topics he stimulated me to investigate, ever seemed to be on the agenda at school, and I had no reason to believe that any of the teachers would even welcome their introduction.

Another version of 'good' teacher is one who waits to be asked. Holt proposed the dictum of *"No question, no teaching"*. Unless someone has asked a question, there is no mandate for teaching. One school, Sudbury Valley in USA takes this seriously, so there is no timetable unless the learners organise or request some systematic learning activity. That this idea alarms or perplexes people tells us how our assumptions about good teaching have been absorbed from a very narrow range of ideas. I saw the 'learners organising the timetable' in action when studying the learning activity of some home-schoolers.

When Robert Owen, who was another person Charlie used to mention, established one of the first infants' schools at New Lanark, he was criticised for his appointment of a particular teacher. He passed over somebody with good literacy skills for a person less proficient. Owen explained the prime requirement for a good teacher, was that *"They were fit company for children."* The more highly qualified person failed his prime requirement.

The next generation of teachers that are needed for the next learning system, however, may well be judged by the Robert Owen requirement. In his book, *In Place of Schools*, (London: New Education Press, 1994), John Adcock predicts that teachers in the future will be quite different from those in the present. They will need to be learning coaches, learning advisers, and learning agents. They will need good interpersonal skills, consultancy skills, and computer research skills, in order to help the members of the families on their case-load 'plan, do, and review', their personal learning programmes. They will need to be *"fit company for learners"*. The skills of crowd control, and crowd instruction that still dominate the behaviour of present day teachers, will not be much in evidence.

2. Crowd instruction: the cop without a uniform

When I trained as a teacher I was introduced to two basic roles. One was that of **crowd-control steward,** since a great deal of time is spent dealing with large groups of conscripted learners. Conscripted learners, like conscripted slaves, are not likely to be automatically pleased about their enforced activity, and therefore need marshalling. As Colin Ward once explained, *"Much of our expenditure on teachers and plant is* *wasted by attempting to teach people what they do not want to learn in a situation that they would rather not be involved in".*

The other basic role was that of **crowd-instructor**. This is having a revival as the current officially favoured method of trying to achieve learning using the formal instruction of groups in classes of anything from 30 -50.

The most impressive crowd-instructor I witnessed personally was the head of the school in which I did my first teaching after college. He would take the whole school of 500 to 600 secondary pupils in the hall for two hours at a time for hymn-singing and mental arithmetic, armed only with a pianist and a cane, so that the staff could complete the end of term reports. Standing on the terraces at the West Bromwich Albion ground one Saturday, I was joined unexpectedly by the head in question. At half-time, after analysing the match for a few minutes, I went on to express my admiration for his performance as a formal teacher with the whole school as his class, and confessed I never saw the day when I could emulate his achievement. His response surprised me. He told me not to be impressed because he had grown to realise that his methods did not lead to much worthwhile education. He said that he appointed young teachers from college in the hope that they would find much better ways than his.

Enthusiasts for the crowd-instructor role ignore the evidence about its inefficiency that I gave previously, where the short-term recall of learners after formal instruction averages 10% with a usual range of 0% to 20%. The long term recall averages 5% with a usual range of 0% to 10 %. You will recall that, as a young teacher, I doubted the evidence and tried various strategies to prove the figures wrong. The pre and post-test results showed again and again that the research was correct. This set in motion my life-long interest in learning systems.

Three other learning systems get better results. These are not the only ones; there are other approaches that help us match the thirty different learning styles we have found in humans. Some promising new approaches are based on computer technology using interactive video and CD-ROM discs.

The first of the three is **purposive conversation** between two and up to eight people. This is one of the reasons that home-based education is so remarkably successful in getting the learners, on average, two years ahead of their schooled counterparts and in some cases, up to ten years ahead. Between 40% and 60% of the time is spent in purposive conversation which replaces the inefficient crowd instruction method. We now know this after over 20 years of research in UK, USA, Canada, Australia and elsewhere.

A second effective learning approach is that of **teaching something to someone else.** This is one of the reasons why people are so easily fooled by formal teaching methods. Because the teacher remembers up to 90% of the material, it is easy to assume that the learners do too. They do not. When they fail to do so, the disappointed teacher cannot face the idea that it is the method that is poor and is likely to blame the learners for being 'lazy' or 'stupid'. It is, of course, the teacher who could be accused of being both lazy and stupid for not reading the research on learning. The explanation for the much-vaunted results of the Pacific-rim countries by the use of formal teaching methods, is in the small print: learners do two hours work with their parents before school and two or more afterwards, **to shore up the inefficiency of the crowd instruction method.** If they followed the example of home-schoolers and cut out the bit in the middle, they might do even better!

A third successful method is that of **learning co-operatives** using the discipline and skills of democratic pedagogy. I was startled to find a considerable leap in standards when I used this approach in teacher education courses. As well as being successful in the standard tasks of memorising and reproducing institutionally approved material, the students also developed an impressive range of bonus skills - resourcefulness, flexibility, curiosity, skill in learning, readiness to unlearn, research techniques and enhanced personal confidence.

They found that they annoyed their alienated fellow learners on other PGCE courses, by their enthusiasm and joy in learning. Colleagues were also known to comment when the students from the learning co-operative attended any of their lecture sessions, that they *"asked an awful lot of questions"*.

Home-schoolers exhibit the same extra bonus skills, and one reason is that the families too, operate as learning co-operatives for periods of time. When students from the learning co-operatives visited families educating at home, they immediately found common ground. So when the famous Harrison case was in court in 1981, they supported the family during the hearing and produced a simulation that they could use in classrooms based on it.

The next learning system, which is only a few years away, and indeed could be in place in months if we had a mind to do it, is unlikely to need either of the roles of crowd control steward or crowd instructor very much. We are, therefore, training teachers for an increasingly obsolete system and creating a cohort of new, young museum-pieces.

The obsolete teachers being produced, are, in the final analysis, being trained as **indoctrinators**. We need to move from working **ON** children, which is the approach of the indoctrinator, to working **WITH** children, which is the approach of the educator. It is time to ignore those who have enthusiasm for the domination-riddled approach of the massive and expensive apparatus of National Curriculum, testing systems and aggressive inspection. Instead, we must learn from the astonishing success of the home-schoolers, about how we might construct a more humane, dignified, and cheaper learning system. Along with this will go a different, enhanced and more professional and worthy role for teachers as learning coaches and consultants rather than crowd control stewards and crowd instructors – 'cops without uniforms', as the USA teacher John Holt used to put it.

3. Head teachers, leadership and courage

Head teachers have featured in the news recently. One reason is that the government has set up a college for head teachers and was looking for a suitable candidate to be in charge. Then, somewhat to my surprise, I found myself addressing three different conferences for head teachers in 1999. In each case I was asked to speak about the next learning system.

Next, a recent conversation I had was about head teachers. A friend observed that he had been to a large meeting in London to hear a head teacher who had made a reputation for turning around so-called failing schools. The head teacher paraded a whole series of aggressive techniques, based on domination, for the approval of the audience. The audience seemed to be impressed. My friend reflected that he seemed to be alone in regarding this head teacher as a licensed institutional bully, with somewhat fascist tendencies and devoid of any democratic ones.

This caused me to reflect on head teachers I admired, and what they had in common. The first head teacher that came to mind was one I have mentioned earlier who, on occasion, would take the whole school of 500 to 600 secondary schoolchildren for two hours a time, for hymn singing and mental arithmetic. I admired his courage in admitting to a young teacher on his staff that that he did not want me to copy him. He said he had learned that his authoritarian methods did not work very well, and he hoped that I would find better ways to do things.

Another head teacher that I met in a Copenhagen school a few years ago, showed another kind of courage. Whereas Denmark has a ratio of one teacher to 18 children, he had manipulated the resources of his school to achieve two teachers to every 18 children. He explained other adventurous ideas operating in his school, and complained bitterly that at 67, he only had three more years to serve before compulsory retirement. One of the visiting party commented, that even for Denmark, some of his initiatives were very daring. He smiled, and said, *"In my experience, it is easier to obtain forgiveness, than it is to obtain permission."* I thought that was the mark of a true innovator.

A different kind of courage was exhibited by a head teacher friend, who having looked into home-based education, decided that this was the appropriate course of action for his two young daughters. He then had to explain to his Governing Body why he thought parents should have such a choice. In a further bout of courage, he later persuaded governors, staff, parents and children, that the education in the school would be much more effective if the school democratised itself. The story is written up in a book, *Participation, Power-sharing and School Improvement*, (Trafford, B., 1998, Educational Heretics Press).

Recently, one head teacher was under siege by the government. Zoe Redhead, staying close to the principles of her father, A.S. Neill, continued to run Summerhill school by encouraging both autonomy and democracy within its walls. Courageously, she refused to submit to the domination-riddled ideas of the inspectors.

I also respect the courage of a secondary head teacher, Philip Toogood, who was put in charge of one of the 'schools of the future' at Telford. He developed it as a campus of small mini- schools working with maximum participation and democracy. Unfortunately, the government of the day had an attack of cold feet regarding the 'schools of the future' initiative. The head teacher resigned in mid-career rather than return the school to the standard authoritarian model. Instead, he joined the Small School at Hartland, then became head of the small parents teacher co-operative school at Ticknall, and then set up the experimental Flexi College in the East Midlands, which moved to Burton-on Trent.

One head teacher, whose courage I admire, I have never met. He is Daniel Greenberg of Sudbury Valley School, U.S.A.

The 'daring' behaviour at Summerhill in allowing children the choice of whether to attend lessons or not, seems mild compared with the approach at Sudbury Valley. Here there is no timetable and no curriculum, until the learners set about devising one. What our domination-riddled OFSTED inspectors would make of this, since they seem reluctant to even tolerate Summerhill, is not hard to imagine. I imagine that they would demand immediate extinction.

I met a head a few years ago who had to cope with the extinction of his school on a regular basis. Piortre ran a school in Poland, in Gdansk, during the Russian occupation. His idea of a good school required a democratic approach with a learner-driven curriculum. The Russian inspectors required the domination-riddled approach of a national curriculum, formal teaching and incessant testing, the model since adopted by OFSTED.

The inspectors sent Piortre to prison and closed his school. The school relocated itself during his absence. The head came out of prison, found the new location and resumed duties. The police came for him again. This happened so often that he decided to have a small suitcase ready packed by the door, so that when the police came in the middle of the night, he could go to his cell without disturbing the family. I think I must give him my top award for courage, but I doubt if he would be regarded as a suitable candidate to run our government's new head teacher college.

The Russians occupying Poland would have approved of the aggressive, authoritarian head teacher applauded for 'turning around failing schools', mentioned earlier. This, of course, raises the question of what counts as good leadership.

The current fashion of describing leadership in terms of the authoritarian model of an 'action man' or 'action woman' contrasts with the democratic view. This has been expressed in these words: *"Of a good leader they say, when the work is done, we did this ourselves."* (after the ancient Chinese philosopher, Lao-Tse)

Dame Patricia Collarbone suggests that a flexible, rotational model of leadership is suitable for the modern world: *"Max De Pree likened leadership to jazz. For me this captures the essence of leadership and learning communities. Jazz bands are collegial. Their members learn from each other, follow each other, lead each other. They are passionate about what they do. They continually experiment, change the rules, take risks. And when it all works, it thrills and excites the participants and the listeners."* (R.S.A. Journal 4/4. 1999.)

Who would I appoint to run a head teachers' college, assuming that I thought such a college was a good idea in the first place? Well, I submit those listed above as suitable candidates. They are all capable people of courage, humanity and democratic in inclination. More practically, those parents who still need to make use of schools have to have some idea of the kinds of heads and teachers they want. Do they stand up to the Robert Owen test, for example, which was, if you recall, *"That they should be fit company for children."*

Part five: superstitions and myths

1. The superstition of socialisation

A study of factors contributing to the development of people of high achievement, who often come to be known as geniuses, was undertaken by H.G.McCurdey at the University of North Carolina, USA. It was reported in George Leonard's book *Education and Ecstasy*, (London: John Murray, 1970). Three factors were identified. One was a high degree of individual attention given by parents and other adults, and expressed in educational activities and accompanied by abundant affection. A second factor was an environment rich in, and supportive of, imagination and fantasy. The third was, **only limited contact with other children,** but plenty of contact with supportive adults.

McCurdey concluded that in mass compulsory schooling, based on formal methods and rigid organisation, we have a long-running experiment in reducing all the above three factors to the minimum. The result is the suppression of high achievement.

Bertrand Russell started his own school at Beacon Hill when he decided that none of the available schools were the kind of places fit for his children, or anybody else's for that matter. He himself had been home-educated. In retrospect, however, he declared that his Beacon Hill school was not as successful as he had hoped. One reason he gave was that he **seriously over-estimated the amount of time children need in the company of each other.**

15,000 hours is a long time to be forced to spend in the company of a selected number of your peers, yet adults persist in declaring that it must be worthwhile socialisation. It may be socialisation, but the **quality** of it is highly suspect. Here are some recent newspaper items that touch on the theme:

Report one: Children now expect bullying to be a regular feature of school life. A national survey commissioned by Family Circle magazine showed that eight out of 10 have suffered at least one sustained attack. On average, the first bullying experience can now be expected at the age of eight.

Report two: A report commissioned by the Suzy Lamplugh Trust showed that weapons on now carried by one in ten school students. We can be relieved that UK is still behind in the international league tables, however, since in the USA, knives and guns are carried by far more students than this. But the trend is upwards and complacency is not justified.

Report three: Primary schools are to be issued drug guidelines by the Head Teachers Association (HTA). Solvent-sniffing is now found to be common amongst children as young as 7. The HTA claimed that schools were choosing to sweep the problem under the carpet by not informing the police, in order to protect the reputation of the school. The peer group in primary schools is now a key source of information about the drugs scene for children in school. Later, as the youngsters grow older, it will supply information about such things as smoking, alcohol, ecstasy tablets, junk food, and expensive teenage fashion.

Report four: The Secretary of State for Education, David Blunkett, launched a crackdown on truancy. He saw it as a 'disengagement from education'. The crackdown was proposed as a measure to combat social exclusion. *"Exclusion from what?"* you might be tempted to ask. *"Weapons, or drugs, or bullying?"*

One of the great supporters of school as socialisation was the USA educationalist John Dewey, but he wanted schools to be **democratic** in style, with high levels of participation and power-sharing, not the totalitarian style based on domination and imposition. The domination model of most of our schools was not part of his plan. He saw the best kind of school as a larger-scale version of the learning approach of the best of the pioneer families of USA.

Yet there is still surprise when a family decides to opt out into home-based education! *"What about the social life?"* they cry. A reply based on the evidence rather than superstition is, ***"Exactly! It is well worth avoiding!"*** Another reply might be that we are a nation of slow learners who cannot work out the significance of report, after report, after report, on the negative socialisation of schooling.

Home-based educating families actually create a much higher quality of social life in their practice of family-centred education, in three ways. First of all, they use the home as a springboard into the community using libraries, museums, and places of interest in both town and country. In the process they rub shoulders with people of all ages. Whilst this is going on, their schooled counterparts are confined to classrooms with a limited range of peers and a limited range of adults.

Secondly, they locate and join groups such as Scouts, Guides, and Woodcraft Folk. They also find groups or classes in judo, swimming and other sports, or natural history and other pursuits.

Thirdly, they seek out other home-schooling families and do things in co-operation. They may be on an occasional basis, or as in the case of more and more groups, on a weekly basis. London thus has the *Otherwise Club* meeting two to three days a week for families to join in if they wish.

But another issue related to the socialisation superstition is discrimination against loners. At parties I have often found myself talking on the side to another person who finds the social attention-seekers getting rather wearing and the endless flow of social trivia getting increasingly boring. I have found that loners often turn out to be more interesting, composed and reflective people and, indeed, some of the most prolific contributors to ideas have been of this disposition. So if your child seems content with their own company - and yours - it is not an automatic cause for concern. Indeed, UK housing policy has just come to terms with the fact that more and more people choose to 'go solo' and this has created a growing demand for single dwellings.

Loners in school can often become the target for bullying because the normal expectation generated by the socialisation superstition, is that you will allow yourself to be taken over by the peer group. This assumes that the artificially created peer group of school is actually worth joining. In the boys grammar school I went to, I judged it was not, and preferred to make my own circle of friends away from the school. Being useful at sports, however, kept me in touch with the peer group without having to be taken over by them. Others were not so lucky.

A head teacher friend provides a final angle on socialisation. He says that the main reason the parents ask for the school to keep its school uniform is because it is protection against the lethal combination of market forces and peer group pressure, which force young people to ask for expensive trainers and other fashion-led items of clothing!

2. The superstition of 'standards'

'Standards' has become one of officialdom's favourite words. But the idea of standards in schooling is both ambiguous and subjective. I will illustrate this with a story. My colleague was in a primary classroom watching a child do the standard achievement tests. The boy was busy colouring in balloons. The test decreed that the more he coloured in, given the time allowed, the higher his supposed achievement. By the end of the test, he had coloured in three, whereas others had coloured in ten or eleven. He spoke to my colleague, sensing a sympathetic ear: *"They say I am slow, but I say I am thorough."* But who says speed is more worthy than thoroughness?

For some, 'standards' means remembering the information designated by adults as 'essential' and therefore enshrined in syllabuses set by complete strangers. Training students to be good at this shallow learning of the selected mechanical tricks of institutionally imposed syllabuses, does not produce the more important deep learning, the kind we need more and more in the future. Shallow learning requires pattern-receiving, whereas deep learning requires pattern-making. Recent research on the brain notes that the brain we are born with is 'wired' or 'programmed' for pattern-making and so young children learn their mother tongue naturally by using this facility and not by the pattern-receiving activity of formal instruction. The brain has to 'rewire' to cope with a regime of constant pattern-receiving and can lose it previous strengths in the process.

Observers like John Holt have concluded that children are less capable as independent learners after years of schooling than they were at the outset, partly because their pattern-making and self-correcting facilities have been eroded. If he is right, we parents need to start thinking carefully about the experiences our children are having.

Indeed shallow learning systems do tend to eradicate the potential to develop deep learning, on the 'if you do not use it, you lose it' principle. The reverse, oddly enough, does not apply. With deep learning habits in your repertoire, you can do shallow learning more or less at will.   With this in mind, some will define 'standards' as standards of deep learning.

Thus Edward de Bono is well known for his advocacy of helping children develop deeper learning, as a first priority. This is part of his reason for declaring all schooling systems known to him as disasters: *"I have not done a full survey or review of education systems around the world so that the views I express are based on personal experience. I would say that all education systems I've had contact with are a disgrace and a disaster."* Is this a Red Alert for us parents when our leaders keep telling us we must keep up with the others?

On the other hand, the character CJ, in The Rise and Fall of Reginald Perrins, used to declare, *"I never got where I am today by thinking."* Which vision do we want for our young, thinking people or gullible ones?

Standards and standardisation are closely related ideas.   The philosopher John Stuart Mill warned us of the trap, as we noted before:

"A general State Education is a mere contrivance for moulding people to be exactly like one another, and as the mould in which it casts them is that which pleases the dominant power in the government, whether this be a monarchy, an aristocracy, or a majority of the existing generation; in proportion as it is efficient and successful, it establishes a despotism over the mind, leading by a natural tendency to one over the body."

Now, this kind of schooling has always appealed to totalitarians. We entered the 19th century with this kind of system and now the government has taken us into the 21st with it, more or less, intact. Yet the Chief Inspector of Schools, Edmond Holmes, was describing this kind of system as the 'tragedy of education' in 1911, and was fired for saying so.

Another objection to the current definition of standards is that most of the required shallow learning is 'junk' knowledge. I define junk knowledge as, 'something you did not need or want to know yesterday, do not need or want to know today, and are unlikely to need or want to know tomorrow'. If you do need or want to know it at sometime, possessing the deep knowledge of such things as questioning, researching and evaluating will enable you to learn it. Indeed, we are all fated to live all our lives in ignorance of most of what is around us because the world of knowledge is now so vast and it is changing all the time.   Without the research skills and some personal confidence derived from practising them, we cannot even make sense of what is necessary to our immediate well-being, and are forced to rely fatalistically on 'experts' who often fail to agree amongst themselves.

Those willing to impose their ideas of standards on others will sooner or later talk about 'the basics'.   But the survivor of a concentration camp had this to say on the matter of basics: *"Reading, writing and arithmetic are important only if they serve to make our children more human."* His eyes had seen the results of a 'high standards' education system - gas chambers built by learned engineers, children poisoned by educated physicians, infants killed by trained nurses, women and babies shot and burned by high school and college graduates. The **manner** of learning is as critical as the learning itself. Learning literacy in a bully institution makes you a literate bully.

But learning to read as early as possible, has become the latest superstition. The contrary view is that learning to read before you have learned to think effectively, just leaves you in a state of gullibility, a sitting duck for propaganda, the simplistic ideas of the tabloids and a multitude of spin doctors. This is why Robert Owen thought that ten-years old was early enough to start the mechanics of reading. By that time the young would have had enough experiences, conversation, debate and exploration to have learnt to think straight. But we do not have to be inflexible about this. Pat Farengo, of the *Growing Without Schooling* group USA, in his address to a London home-education conference, explained that his daughters had all learnt to read at different ages, one early, one about the common age of seven years, and another several years later. As a home-based educator, he was able to be flexible and stay cool about these individual differences.

Another basic we are asked to accept is the superiority of ruthless, competitive behaviours. Our leaders keep telling us that the next century requires this of us and have insisted that it be the first aim of schooling. Nat Needle, a US writer responds: *"... if the 21st century becomes the story of human beings around the world pitted against each other in a struggle for well-being, even survival, this will only be because we failed to imagine something better and insist on it for ourselves and our children."*
In contrast to the view that the victors in the 'strong versus weak' battle deserve our adulation for setting the pace for the rest of us, Needle reminds us of another view. It is that the strongest are those who devote themselves to strengthening the weak, to keeping the whole community afloat, to ploughing their gifts back into the common field through service to others. He concludes: *"I don't care to motivate my children by telling them that they will have to be strong to survive the ruthless competition. I'd rather tell them that the world needs their wisdom, their talents, and their kindness, so much so that the possibilities for a life of service are without*

limits of any kind. I'd like to share with them the open secret that this is the path to receiving what one needs in a lifetime, and to becoming strong."

This extract from a recent *Living Green* journal adds to this an alternative to relentless consumerism - the virtues of 'living lightly' - by saying: *"Try to live simply. A simple lifestyle freely chosen is a source of strength. Do not be persuaded into buying what you do not need or cannot afford. Do you keep yourself informed about the effects your style of living is having on the global economy and environment?"*

In the first part of this century, Bertrand Russell observed: *"We are faced with the paradoxical fact that education has become one of the chief obstacles to intelligence and freedom of thought."* Since the model of education he described is the same as the one we still have, in all key respects, we parents and grandparents have to ask whether we are having imposed on us entirely the wrong standards.

3. Some educational superstitions of our time - Shakespeare, Maths and Handwriting

Professor S. Bengu, former Minister of Education for South Africa, gave a keynote speech at a conference on democratic education in1997. In it explained his country's intention to move away from a bureaucrat-driven imposed curriculum towards a **learner-driven** curriculum by 2005.

The enthusiasts for imposing a curriculum on the learners are often horrified at such heresy. *"What if the learners do not choose to learn Shakespeare?"* I always thought that Bertrand Russell gave the cool answer here, when he said: *"Shakespeare did not write with a view to boring school-children; he wrote to with a view to delighting his audiences. If he does not give you delight, you had better ignore him."*

I always found comfort in this view, since I admit that, despite many visits to performances at Stratford-on-Avon, I can take or leave the bard. This does not mean I want to stand in the way of those who want to encounter Shakespeare, and for this reason, I find that the work of John and Leela Hort in making the language of his plays intelligible, is well worth both parents and children investigating. With their love of the bard, Leela and John have spent their time and money producing the *Inessential Shakespeare* series, 'shortened and simplified versions in modern English', a snip at £3-95 each. Six plays have been translated into modern English so far, and the seventh, Julius Caesar, is in preparation.

The enthusiasts for imposing a curriculum on the learners are also worried by Maths. *"What if the learners do not choose to learn Mathematics?"* Bertrand Russell, who should have a valid opinion since he was one of the world's most renowned mathematicians himself, had this to say on the matter:

"In universities, mathematics is taught mainly to men who are going to teach mathematics to men who are going to teach mathematics to ... Sometimes, it is true, there is an escape from this treadmill. Archimedes used mathematics to kill Romans, Galileo to improve the Grand Duke of Tuscany's artillery, modern physicists (grown more ambitious) to exterminate the human race. It is usually on this account that the study of mathematics is commended to the general public as worthy of State support."

Maths is useful, however, if you are doing something like designing bridges, but the idea that we must all go through the Maths experience to identify those who are good at it and need it later for specific tasks, is about as sound as saying we must all study dentistry to enable some expert dentists to emerge. When I was learning Maths at school, then teaching it in school myself, and then watching my son learn it, the same heretical thought kept occurring, that surely there are better things we could all be doing than this stuff.

It is a common error to confuse mathematics with arithmetic, and so perhaps it is the latter that should be imposed? Again, Russell is a dissenter: *"Arithmetic ... is overvalued; in British elementary schools and it takes up far more of the time than it should."* He goes on to propose that there are much more useful things to learn. Russell admitted that although he was a leading mathematician and philosopher, he was never much good at arithmetic himself.

It is another common error to think industry has 'needs' that can be 'covered'. A colleague who was a Maths tutor, conducted a survey of the 'needs' of hundreds of firms around Birmingham. When I asked him what he had found, he said, *"Total confusion."* He could not find any common requirements in mathematics, and the common ground as regards arithmetic amounted to knowledge and confidence in the four basic rules. This squares with my own experience because when I left school at 16 and went work in a bank, my 'O' level Maths proved to be pretty useless and I had to learn the number games of the bank on the spot.

One home-educating family, where the father was an engineer, asked me at a conference what to do about Maths. I ran through the arguments. They decided it **was** a superstition, and to have the courage to ignore it unless it cropped-up in the course of other investigations. Later they said how pleased they were with this policy and how well it had worked out in practice. But then, with CD-ROM interactive discs now available that will teach you 'O' level Maths in half or less of the time of a taught course, you can take the subject on board whenever you wish.

If I believed in compelling people to learn things, which I no longer do, since I advocate the learner-driven/catalogue curriculum/natural curriculum approach instead, I could make out a much better case for teaching Logic, which is usually missing from the curriculum altogether. But it was Paul Goodman, in a book that shocked people in 1962 entitled, *Compulsory Mis-education,* (Harmondsworth: Penguin), who described mass schooling, including its imposed mathematics, as a mass superstition.

The enthusiasts for imposing a curriculum on the learners are also worried by joined-up handwriting. *"What if the learners do not choose to learn joined-up handwriting?"* I must admit to being much more worried if they do not develop the skills of joined-up thinking that learning logic encourages, but that is another issue. Perhaps more pain is inflicted on children in the joined-up handwriting pursuit than any other. Yet printers print in script, because it is clearer. *Natural Parent* would be hard work to read if it were presented in handwriting.

Nobody shows much enthusiasm for joined-up figures in sums either, and would see anyone as a bit odd for suggesting it. John Holt in his investigations could find no reasons on offer except a claim that joined-up handwriting was speedier. He showed that this usually was a fallacy by conducting a number of classroom experiments and by experimenting on himself. Usually, script was as quick or often quicker, more legible and looked better. Those who chose to learn Italic script produced very attractive results.

In discussion recently, one handwriting enthusiast told me that the body movements used in the teaching of it were essential for the composed development of children. This was her justification for teaching handwriting. If this is so, why not teach the body movements on their own without the clutter?
The enthusiasts for imposing learning on children in school do not have a good track record. There were earlier super-stitions. For a time they tried to make all left-handed children become right-handed, with a heavy punishment regime. Drill was imposed as a subject on all children for many years. Children in Welsh-speaking areas of Wales were punished if they did not speak in English in school. Later compulsory Welsh appeared in English-speaking parts of Wales and I have met adults who resented this being enforced on them as children. And so on.

Part of the task of 'parents as researchers' that I have advocated, is to be on the look-out for learning systems based on possible superstitions and get equipped to answer them and deal with them.

The Inessential Shakespeare Series is available from 239 Bramcote Lane, Wollaton, Nottingham NG8 2QL Telephone 0115 928 3001 for a brochure.
See web-site www.startingshakespeare.com

4. Dyslexia and the obsession with literacy

A few years ago, I invited trainee teachers to visit home-educating families to see what they might learn from such an experience. One young woman visited a family where all four children, two boys and two girls, were diagnosed by the unit at the University of Aston as dyslexic in varying degrees of severity.

The trainee teacher herself had a first-class honours degree from Oxford University. Yet in her written evaluation of her day spent with the family she wrote that the children made her feel completely uneducated. How could this be? She would be described conventionally as highly educated because she was highly literate.

She explained that for every academic skill she possessed, they had three or four practical skills. They could, amongst other things, grow their own food, make their own clothes, cook and bake, keep bees, dismantle and rebuild cars and service them, put a roof on a house, build walls, install central heating systems, milk goats, and keep hens. They could also talk to her about her political studies of pressure groups because they were active in groups such as *Friends of the Earth.*

The parents had adopted an unusual approach to the dyslexia of the children. It was 'accentuate the positive and ignore the negative'. They had a learning approach that concentrated on activities that children could do with success and left aside reading and writing to develop later.

 Years later, all are competent, composed and flexible adults whose company is most agreeable. They can turn their hands to a variety of ways of earning money. They can all cope with reading and writing with varying degrees of achievement. One is fluent, and three are competent, despite a warning from the Aston University Unit that one, possibly two, might never learn to read.

The response of the trainee teacher about feeling uneducated raises some important issues. Has literacy, in the form of reading and writing, become an obsession or even a superstition? John Holt made this observation:

"From the fuss we make about reading, one might think that this was a country of readers, that reading was nearly everyone's favourite or near favourite pastime. Who are we kidding? A publisher told me not long ago that outside of 300 or so college bookstores there are less than 100 true bookstores in all the United States."

George Trevelyan observed that, *"Education has produced a vast population able to read but unable to distinguish what is worth reading."* His point is supported by the finding that the best-selling newspapers are tabloids with a reading age of about 11 years.

The time and effort spent on teaching reading also flies in the face of the facts that it usually takes about 30 hours to learn, provided that it takes place in a learner-friendly environment. This figure comes from Paulo Freire's work with illiterate peasants in South America where he logged the progress of cohort after cohort of reading classes. Those home-based educators who have also logged progress, report similar results. If it takes longer it can be because inhibitions have been built in by the learning situation. The more time devoted to forcing the pace, the greater the opportunity cost, so that the skills the dyslexic family had gained, that so impressed the trainee teacher, are squeezed out. In any case, illiteracy is a common experience: we are all illiterate when we arrive in foreign countries. Yet we manage to cope, using our intelligence and benefiting from the help and tolerance of the natives.

In the end, however, we come back to the main reason for literacy. The economic motive of 'for the good of the economy', which is constantly stressed by governments, did not impress the survivor of a concentration camp, as mentioned before. Here is his letter, in full:

"Dear Teacher,
I am a survivor of a concentration camp. My eyes saw what no man should witness:

Gas chambers built by learned engineers,
Children poisoned by educated physicians
Infants killed by trained nurses,
Women and babies shot and burned by high school and college graduates.

So I am suspicious of education.

My request is: Help your students become human. Your efforts must never produce learned monsters, skilled psychopaths, educated Eichmans.

Reading, writing and arithmetic are important only if they serve to make our children more human."

Finally, recent technology has come to the aid of many dyslexic people. Voice-driven computers have been shown to be effective in 90% of the cases in the research undertaken by Aptech Ltd who have developed the software in this country. Indeed, the arrival of voice recognition technology is likely to move us gently and inevitably into a new oracy age.

This technology breaks the domination of print literacy. Of course, books and other reading material will still be useful and will not disappear, but their domination is gone. Machines can read and write for us. This can be occasionally, or most of the time, or all of the time, just as we choose and according to the situation.

To some extent the decline of the use of print for information and entertainment has already started and has been replaced by TV and radio, for more and more adults and children. The development of advanced telephone technology, including the arrival of mobile telephones, has already had the effect of moving activities away from the print literacy skills into more use of oral skills. An obvious example is the growth of telephone banking.

Next, the arrival of book-reading technology for blind people, is equally usable by the sighted with reading difficulties. There are more developments to come, such as the use of virtual reality and the next generation of wallet-size computers.

Thus, the move from an era of the domination of print-based literacy into a new era where oral literacy will be more central, is already under way, even if its significance has not yet been widely recognised. As a case in point, this article was written, (or should it be 'voiced'?) using, *Dragon Naturally Speaking* software supplied by Aptech. I find it to be a kind of magic when you see your voice turned into accurate print, and I am not dyslexic. For those with dyslexia, it must seem like a liberation.

5. You become what you read?

You will recall that it usually takes about 30 hours to learn the mechanics of reading, according to Paulo Freire, based on his work with adult literacy schemes in a variety of countries. This is confirmed in the experience of various home-based educators, though some would say it can take up to 60 hours with children.

If learning to read takes longer than 60 hours, or fails altogether, there are several possible reasons. The first is that the learning situation is learner-hostile. A second is that the learner is not yet motivated to learn to read and has been forced to learn too early. A third is that the learner is dyslexic.

As noted earlier, Robert Owen inclined to the view that children should not be troubled with the mechanics of reading until they were about ten years of age. Until then they should be engaged in collecting a wide range of experiences of the world and in purposive conversation and debate, to develop their powers of critical thinking. In modern psychological terms, they were to develop deep learning of understanding before the shallow learning of mechanical operations.

Rudolph Steiner, on the other hand, was inclined to think that the age of seven was appropriate. The current orthodoxy is to start much earlier than this, ignoring the evidence that this risks early failure, feelings of inadequacy, and a general reaction against learning.

Alan Thomas, in his recent book, *Educating Children at Home*, (London: Cassell, 1998), indicates how many home-educating families experience a variety of ages of starting to read amongst the children, and have the flexibility to cope with it positively. Parents, however, need the courage to resist any current orthodoxy, and also to deal with their own anxieties.

My own son learnt to read early, and when he chose to try school at five years of age, he already had a reading age of twelve. I was, at the time, somewhat anxious that he had learnt to read 'too early', but not foolish enough to have discouraged him.

A colleague who had the same 'problem' told me how the head teacher had thrown up her hands in horror, and told him that he and his wife had completely ruined his daughter's infant school experience by allowing her to read early. The disease of orthodoxy can strike in many forms!

Another current orthodoxy is to promote the teaching of reading by phonics, often confusing two variations, synthetic and analytical approaches, as the one right away. When my son was learning to read, I was also running reading workshops for young student teachers, and laid due stress on the need to pay attention to phonics, as did everyone I knew who was training teachers at the time.

My son took to the *Breakthrough to Literacy* approach to reading with its personal word folders and personal word-building folders - this last being the analytical phonics element of the scheme. My son was politely but persistently dismissive of the word-building folder, and seemed to think this was a device to hold him back. He just wanted to know what any new word said and he would memorise it.

From this experience, I began to learn to be more cautious about the use of phonics. After all, although Esperanto has a 100% rating for phonetic regularity, English only rates about 40%. In other words, as regards English, you are asked to learn a rule, and then often have to learn all the many exceptions to it.

Another note of caution sounded when a colleague who went blind demonstrated his new reading machine to me. He would open a book, place it on the machine which would then read it to him. He explained that the development of the machine had been held up for several years because they tried to use a phonics-based approach. As a result, the machine could not attain fluency.

Only when they switched to whole word recognition approach, with phonics as emergency backup to attack unfamiliar words, did the machine gain fluency. The machine appeared to be in sympathy with my son!

A recent experience has reconfirmed my caution. I began to learn Esperanto, an entirely phonetically regular language. In consequence I can read out loud to you a whole page of the language, but have only a partial understanding of what I have performed so convincingly.

It may be that the general obsession with reading is becoming dated. The sale of books in the USA is in decline as more and more people get the information they need by electronic means. This includes television, radio, video, and telephone. Mobile telephones that link you to a data-bank, that then talks the information back to you, are increasingly becoming part of our experience. Telephone banking is but one example of this. Another is telephoned directory enquiries, and the telephone speaking clock has been with us for many years.

As I am write this text with a voice-driven computer, I am aware that with an additional piece of software, the computer would read it back to me, to save me the chore of reading the screen. A long-standing friend who is severely dyslexic, Geoff Harrison, has been liberated by this technology, and has spent some time helping edit a magazine.

Looking ahead, the flight deck of the Star Ship *Enterprise*, does not utilise reading because all decisions are based on voice-dialogue with the ship's computer.   The commander might be dyslexic - it would be of no consequence.

We are moving steadily into a new age of oracy.   Reading will continue to be useful, and for many a source of enjoyment, but probably less and less decisive.   Even now, the gypsy culture in our midst manages without reliance on reading.   We, ourselves, as pointed out previously, are often illiterate the moment we set foot in a foreign country, but somehow we get by.

We can often forget the dangers of reading.   You can easily become what you read.   If your reading does not go beyond the tabloid newspaper level, you become enslaved to the tabloid mentality, which has been described as superstitious, dogmatic, nationalistic and inclined towards racism, sexism and ageism.

This idea was explored in full in Richard Hoggart's book, *The Uses of Literacy*, (Harmondsworth: Penguin).   Unless learners have developed the skills and habits of discrimination, or 'crap detection', as Postman and Weingartner put it their book, *Teaching as a Subversive Activity,* (Harmondsworth: Penguin, 1971), they are at the mercy of self-interested persuaders.   Most learners pass out of school just literate enough to be conned, to be spun by the spin doctors, and to watch the more mindless shows on television.

We need to go way beyond mere mechanical literacy, to critical literacy.   This means that people learn to see through the linguistic, semantic, intellectual and other deceptions which now dominate our culture.

Hoggart restated his points in a *Guardian Education* article (2nd December 1997):

"In a democracy, people have a right to read the Sun, and only the Sun, if they wish. But would you be happy if, by the time your own children and grown-up, they too 'read' only the Sun, watched only the more idiotic television programmes for almost 40 hours a week and, if they bothered with books at all, read-only formulaic market fodder? The founding principal of critical literacy ... must be to develop understanding of the nature of democracy itself, of the duties it lays on us and the rights we may then claim; the two are inseparable."

Hoggart is not impressed by the results of the reading industry so far: *"But the great majority, insofar as they read at all, go round and round, wooed on to that carousel of repetitive rubbish ceaselessly operated by the two-syllabled press and the stereotyped paperbacks."*

Perhaps Robert Owen was less zany than we might think in wanting to leave the mechanics of reading until much later and develop the powers of critical thinking first.

Part six: Visions of the next learning system

Introduction

Part six is made up of three particular visions about the next learning system. It is important to note that the impression sometimes given in the media is that 'there is no other way' other than mass coercive schooling, is false. Soft censorship has been applied to any alternative ideas i.e. by not reporting them, or by dismissing them in distorted 'sound-bites'.

But there have been several viable alternative visions around over the last century. Amongst these are Henry Morris and the Community College concept. Earlier there was Charlotte Mason and her 'sane education' based on the notion that 'teachers should teach less so that scholars should learn more'. Then the Chief Inspector for Schools at the start of the 20th century, Edmond Holmes, advocated diversity and variety in place of the uniformity he supervised for 15 years in the first National Curriculum. He grew to recognise the latter as the 'tragedy of education'. More recently, there was the flexi-schooling alternative to the day detention centre model of schooling I proposed myself.

Now there is the development of all-age personalised and community learning centres arising from the growth of the home-based education alternative. *Creating Learning Communities,* edited by Ron Miller, and *Creating a Cooperative Learning Centre, an idea-book for home schooling families,* by Katherine Houk, are featured in the third part as representative of this vision.

Meanwhile, California State is in the process of adopting a complete revision of the comprehensive school vision to provide *'alternatives for everybody all the time'*, rather than the uniformity of the *'one size fits all'* mistakes of the past.

1. Teaching tomorrow

My choice for education book of the year 2000 was *Teaching Tomorrow: personal tuition as an alternative to school*, (Nottingham: Education Now, 2000), with its vision of a new teaching profession that serves families and their learning plans, rather than dictating to them.   Here is my interview with its author, John Adcock.

Roland: In your books you see a close, trusting partnership between parent and teacher as the cornerstone of successful childhood education?

John: Yes, but as the child gets older he or she will join that decision-making partnership and contribute increasingly to the plans being drawn up for his or her education. I'm talking here of the early-education stage from birth to 13 or l4 years - and even before that, because most parents welcome advice on coming to terms with the changes that will occur in their lives after their baby is born. My wife and I certainly did! Then, as well as pre-natal support, they will need practical help and a whole range of ideas for encouraging and stimulating the learning processes that begin in their child's earliest days.

Roland: Long before he or she reaches the age of five when school starts?

John: Yes - except that 'school', in the way that word has been under-stood over the past 130 years, becomes an increasingly irrelevant concept as we enter the 21st century. But not only irrelevant: with some children - perhaps many - the school, as now constituted, can become an obstacle to much learning. Economic, social and technological change has been so rapid and all-embracing since 1945 that we can now be thinking radically of an education system for young people in which the traditional school plays no part at all. I think we have reached a critical stage in state-provided education and need, rather urgently, as many novel and thought-provoking ideas as we can get.

Roland: Getting a hearing for major new ideas is not easy, as we both know well.

John: Far from it! For instance, when state schooling for five-year-olds began in the 1870s no practical alternative forms of teaching were available. Now exciting alternatives are here already. The social significance is truly immense - but little media time is given to that. Concern is restricted to ways of keeping the 19th century system on the road! Back in Victorian times, however, many parents and grandparents were semi-illiterate, their homes crowded, their spare time and money non-existent, their teaching resources meagre, and technological help was nearly a century away. A family-based education, as opposed to a school-based one, was a non-starter - except for the rich. Children had to be taken from their homes and taught in schools. And fairly forbidding places most of them were!

But the situation of families in Britain today is beyond anything even dreamt of by the average parent of 1870. Today, the possibilities for educating children at home, each according to his need, are infinite. More space, time, money, knowledge and other resources, all combined with limitless, but controlled, support from the multimedia, makes possible an enjoyable, encouraging and personalised study programme, with skilled individual tuition, for every boy and girl.

No longer do we need classes of 30 pupils, in schools of hundreds, following a politically-contrived, centrally-administered, imposed and externally-inspected national curriculum, based on the targets, tests, performance league tables, and the naming and shaming antics so beloved of the civil servants and politicians in their London-based offices.

Roland: So, it isn't the school as such which you object to, but rather what goes on inside it? What the children and teachers are subjected to and what the parents are persuaded to believe is important?

John: That's the whole point. And that is what must be made clear. After 3O years working in state education, I know how hard most children work, how supportive most parents are, how conscientious most teachers are, and how seriously most school governors take their duties. Much work is done in schools which is good and it would be ridiculous and hurtful to say otherwise. But it is the institution of school - its rigid social structure - with its physical restrictions, large numbers, time-tabling requirements, disciplinary code, hierarchical set-up, standardised curriculum, tests, inspections and stress that is the problem.

Think how much more a gifted teacher could do if she were wholly trusted and given free rein to spend her time, her energy, her imagination and her other resources. - as well as her compassion - to devise work schemes for her pupils, aided by their parents, working in small study groups at different times and places as agreed. The school as we know it would become superfluous and the vast sums spent on its upkeep could be released for more valuable, personalised educational work.

Roland: But what of the billions. already invested in school land and buildings and in our huge teaching force?

John: Some buildings would continue to be used - but not as schools. After conversion some would become vital community resource centres offering libraries, sports centres, laboratories, recreation areas, study sections, cafes, health advisory services, overnight accommodation, multimedia facilities and much more. They would be open to all local residents. Some strategically-placed schools would become field-centres.

As regards existing teachers, those who wanted to, and who were prepared to retrain, would become personal, professional family tutors to small groups of children and their parents. They would be there to help all those parents who wanted to plan and then see through the early education of their own children.

Roland: The education of the child would pass to the family?

John: It would pass *back* to the family. For thousands of years the family, several generations of it, educated its own children. Universal and compulsorily-attended schools changed that, during a particular and unlikely-to-be-repeated period of economic development in western society in the late 19th century. That period has passed. Now the family, benefiting from the huge opportunities that period eventually gave rise to, can resume its original work. The school will be seen as a blip in recent social history: no more.

Given the extraordinary resources readily available, the key to the new approach will be maximum trust. Trust at all times. Trust between child, parent and personal tutor. That trust is imperative in all professional relationships, and it will be in the new profession of tutoring. There will be the recognition that all children and their family circumstances are different: that they are unique, and that it follows that sets of needs are different too, so that the designing of a successful early-education programme for a child will depend on the recognition and acceptance of those differences. Parents are likely to know of these needs in their own children earlier and sense them more deeply than the personal tutor, and parents' input in the construction of each study programme will be essential.

Roland: But some needs might be common to a sizeable majority of children?

John: Yes, such as the learning of sound health practices, of having opportunities for establishing valuable social relationships, for the acquiring of literacy and numeracy, for internalising compassion and an understanding of others. We know that children differ physically, and that their potential for development in many areas is varied, as is their increasing range of interests. The task for personal tutors and parents will be, gradually and patiently, not only to construct and then amend programmes of study, but to carry them through in many different environments. It will be a challenging role, but one that will be greatly rewarding in the work satisfaction gained.   The child will be happily involved, the parent directly involved, and the tutor professionally involved.

Roland: But all this is demanding much of the tutor. Can she succeed?

John: There are two points there. It is, no doubt, asking a lot of the tutor, but just think of what we now ask of a general medical practitioner!   The tutor will get the same level of training and accept the *same* level of responsibility as the family doctor - perhaps more. In return, society must give her the same level of resources, respect and reward.

Can she do it? Yes: with help. First through her long, demanding initial professional training, and then, throughout her career, by means of generous study leave. Those teachers who feel they cannot or do not want to undertake this new role should be offered alternative, less taxing, work. But no personal tutor will be working on her own: there will be no classroom whose door will close, leaving her with 30 unresponsive pupils. Panels of seven or eight tutors will cover the age range 0 to 13 years and so each will be able to consult with the others and specialise, to some extent, with a chosen age group.

She will be aided by reconstituted university departments of education and by ever more powerful multimedia libraries. Also, her role will be very different from that of the schoolteacher: the bulk of 'lesson' material will be freely available from the multimedia on demand - anywhere at any time. Part of the tutor's skill will lie in knowing what is available, sourcing it, assessing and amending it, and cleverly incorporating it into the programme of study which has been devised for her pupil and accepted by his parents. The parallel with the GP and her patients, group practice, technology and teaching hospital resources, continues to hold good. Indeed, we could be seeing, during this century, a merging or working-together of education and medicine!

Roland: Then, on top of all that, you advocate in your new book, *Teaching Tomorrow,* the payment of a salary to some parents?

John: Certainly. To those parents who choose to train for and qualify in the increasingly-demanding and socially important craft of parenthood and who stay at home, full-time, to educate - with the tutor's help - their young children. Yes, and it would be a substantial amount. There is no more important work in our society than caring for the next generation. We need to ensure that every pound or dollar spent is well spent, and we cannot claim that is the case in the system today.

If this seems revolutionary, remember that taking children from home to school - compulsorily - was just such a revolution in the 1870s. In 2000 we could be into counter-revolution. We need no longer see childhood education devised for employers' and nations' benefits, but for children's benefit - aiming for a more considerate, less competitive, less grasping, less consumer-based future. Childhood education will be in the hands of parents and tutors rather than those of politicians and their bureaucrats. Politicians may not like that, but in my view, that is all to the good: the less they have to do with our children's education the better!

* * * * *

Teaching Tomorrow: personal tution as an alternative to school (ISBN 1.871526.44.2 published by Education Now) costs £9-95 (or £19-95 in hardback ISBN 1.871526.46.9) p.&.p. included,   from Education Now, 113 Arundel Drive, Bramcote Hills, Nottingham

2. Roland Meighan interviews Sir Christopher Ball

(Sir Christopher Ball is currently Chancellor of the University of Derby and a former Director of the Campaign for Learning.)

Roland: Why do you think learning is so important?

Christopher: Doesn't everybody? Human learning is the source of health, wealth and happiness. It offers each one of us our best hope of living a good, fulfilled life and finding work that is both worthwhile and rewarding. I like to imagine that for at least two millennia Europe's great project has been the creation of a good society. Of course, others have the same project - and Europe has made many mistakes in the pursuit of social welfare. But the idea of a good society has never been lost to view. For a long time Europeans thought that religion was the key. We believed that a common faith was a prerequisite for a good society. Many people died as a result. Then politics gradually came to replace religion as 'the big idea' which would enable us to create a good society. More people died. We live now at the very end of the political era. And still the fundamental question remains to be answered: where can we find the authority and foundation upon which to construct the good society, if religion and politics are inadequate? I believe the solution lies in the learning individual. Each of us has the capacity to learn to live well, work effectively and help at last to create the good society of which people have dreamed for so long. Learning is fundamental to human progress.

Roland: If that is so, what are the obstacles that prevent people learning?

Christopher: I used to think that the major impediments to learning were lack of opportunities and low intelligence. I have changed my mind. I now believe that the real problems are self-esteem, confidence and motivation. Successful learning requires four things - that learners feel good about themselves, really want to learn, have the capacity to succeed, and find access to good opportunities for learning. Important as the latter two are, I have come to think that anyone blessed with self-esteem, confidence and motivation will find the capacity within themselves to succeed in their chosen field of learning, and will discover and secure the opportunities they need to make progress. Intelligence is not in short supply: nor are educational opportunities. But even successful people have problems with self-esteem, confidence and motivation. The rest are partially disabled by the lack of these qualities. What interests me today are the attitudes exemplified by statements like: 'I'm no good... I couldn't do it... I couldn't care less'. Where do such attitudes come from? How can we prevent or correct them? How can we promote self-esteem, confidence and motivation in all children and every adult?

Roland: Good question! How can we?

Christopher: I believe that the instinct to learn is innate, like the instincts to breathe or suck. We are born feeling good about ourselves, programmed to develop self-esteem, confidence and motivation, provided the appropriate developmental environment is there. We need nourishment and stimulation. No-one doubts today the importance of good food for the growing child. The stimulation provided by 'warm, demanding adults' is even more important for successful development. High-achievers appear to share three critical factors in their early development: plenty of contact with warm, demanding adults, an exploratory curriculum of learning, and only limited access to the peer group. So, if you want to blame someone for low self-esteem, lack of confidence or poor motivation round up the usual suspects - parents, teachers and the peer group! I would rather encourage them to provide the conditions for successful development, an environment characterised by 'high challenge' coupled with 'low threat'. The following matrix schematically demonstrates the effects on the learning child or adult of different combinations of challenge and threat.

	high challenge	low challenge
high threat:	anxious :	dim

low threat: bright   :   spoilt

In practice, home schooling at its best comes closest to getting these things right, and fosters children's self-esteem, confidence and motivation as a result. Of course, schools, colleges and universities can do it too. But they find it more difficult to satisfy the three critical factors I have identified. 'Outdoor education' (of the kind offered by *Brathay Hall* or *Outward Bound*) provides a good example of my idea of best practice, as does *Landmark Education* (ring 0171-969-202020 for details).

Roland: Do you think learning and development are the same thing?

Christopher: No. I like to distinguish between 'natural development' and 'artificial education'. It is natural to learn to walk and talk - everyone does it, unless they are most severely disabled or extremely deprived of normal stimulation. Even bad homes cannot prevent natural development, though they can retard and stunt it. It is unnatural (or artificial) to learn Latin or trigonometry - or, indeed, to read and write. Artificial education needs teachers who can inspire, motivate, demonstrate and instruct. Those who champion child-centred learning are right in the case of natural development. No-one needs to be taught how to walk and talk. Those who believe in teacher-led learning are right about artificial education. Everyone needs help to become literate. Natural development and artificial education are easy to distinguish at the extremes, but they merge in the centre. Fighting is natural; football artificial. Sex and play are both. It is part of being human to weave together our natural and cultural inheritance. Those whose business it is to promote learning (of both kinds) should be aware of the different demands of the two forms of learning I have distinguished, and know when to encourage natural development and when to provide artificial education. Good parents and teachers do just that.

Roland: Do you think the existing provision for education and training is sustainable in this new century?

Christopher: No and yes! It is certainly not sustainable if you mean by that 'satisfying the learning needs of the whole community'. The National Commission on Education reported a few years ago that some 20% of adults and school-leavers had difficulties with numeracy, and some 15% with literacy, such that they found it difficult to find and keep a job. This is a very disappointing outcome after more than 120 years of compulsory, free, elementary education. Attitudes to schooling tell the same story. *The Campaign for Learning's* survey of 1996 revealed that 17% or one in six adults and children did not enjoy learning at school. This isn't good enough. I can't believe that human ingenuity is incapable of inventing better arrangements for the education and training of the young. As a first step, I suggest that governments should offer parents a choice between three forms of provision - full-time schooling, part-time schooling (coupled with home education) and home schooling - and make the choice real by funding each mode appropriately. But, sadly, I see little prospect of serious change at present. When I was in the army, I learned that one should 'reinforce success'. The nation (and its governments of either persuasion) seems instead to be intent on reinforcing a failing system at present. High achievers are fostered by plenty of warm, demanding adults, an exploratory curriculum and limited access to the peer-group. Class sizes of 30+, the rigid and overloaded National Curriculum, and age-related education are all inappropriate forms of provision to encourage everyone to learn and achieve their highest potential. It is no use tinkering with our 19th century model of education: it needs to be completely rethought and restructured. Gradual reform is unlikely to succeed. Radical change is what is required.

Roland: What factors do you think will shape the learning system of the future?

Christopher: ICT, brain-science and vouchers! The impact of Information and Communications Technology is still in its infancy. But I see ICT as a new learning technology, not a supplementary aid for the classroom. While not as significant as the invention of writing, I expect it to have an even greater impact than printing. The marriage of the computer and television will connect every home at low cost to the world's store of knowledge in a convenient and accessible way. The ICT market will progressively lower the costs, raise the quality, and increase the convenience of this form of provision for learning at home (or at work). Just as the motor-car challenged the railways, so ICT will challenge the monopoly of the classroom mode and the public service of education.

The cognitive and neuro-sciences are on the threshold of a real breakthrough in the understanding of the brain. It will not be long before we master the biology of learning, the nature of intelligence and the processes of memory. A biological theory of learning will provide a new basis from which to derive a rational practice of education. Some things are already obvious. If you want children to learn a second language, teach it in primary schools.

Socialisation and team-work are mastered in the nursery. People have different styles of learning. No-one reaches their full potential. Our feelings control our learning. And so on. 'Vouchers' is a politically loaded term for a simple idea. I am not in favour of reducing the public spending on education - though I doubt whether it needs to be increased very much. What we need to do is to focus our public spending on early learning - nursery and primary education, and the support of parents. I like to quote the 'RSA rule' for the public funding of a service of education: 'Calculate the appropriate class-size (or student-teacher ratio) by doubling the age of the learner, so that 3 year-olds would be six to an adult, 6 year-olds in classes of twelve, and so on'. As people mature into adulthood they need less not more social support and private funding can come to the aid of the reduced public provision - as is already beginning to happen in higher education. None of this is what is meant by 'vouchers'. Voucher-funding, like the idea of Individual Learning Accounts, means the distribution of public funding to the (potential) learners, rather than to those who provide education. Fund the learner, not the teaching, and create a sort of educational market where learners (and their parents) can exercise choice to improve quality and convenience and reduce cost.

These three concepts, given free rein, will bring about the radical change we need. The first two (ICT and brain-science) are unstoppable. The third requires a braver government than we have at present.

Roland: What are your own learning plans?

Christopher: As I have already indicated, I am fascinated by topics like leadership, literacy and the human brain. I shall never become an expert in these fields, but I am trying to acquire a good general knowledge of them: As for skills, I should like to learn how to become a better cook, more effective fund-raiser, faster solver of The Times crossword puzzle... The Third Age is a good time of life, provided you keep your health.   Becoming a grandfather is at one and the same time an education and a challenge.   I wish one could register for an NVQ in grandparenthood! But qualifications seem less important now than competence. This is a time of life when one revives old interests, or explores new ones, such as (in my case) drawing, dancing, singing and long-distance walking.   Knowledge, skills - and attitudes (KSA). The third is the most important. Indeed, I prefer the idea of an ASK Curriculum. I shall continue my 'Landmark Education' with a six-month Introduction to Leadership Programme, after which I hope to have gone a long way towards resolving the problems of self-esteem, confidence and motivation for myself - and be ready to enrol others into the learning society!

3. Learning centres instead of schools?

(OR: Why not scrap schools and replace them with something more humane, more intelligent and more up-to-date?)

We have all just witnessed an astonishing event. We have gone into a new century with the same model of education with which we started the old century – the 'tell them and test them' model. It is rather like basing modern transport policy on the coach and horses. What makes it more astonishing is that the Chief Inspector of Schools at the start of the last century, Edmond Holmes, spent thirty years trying to make the model work efficiently, (including its 'payment by results' approach now re-born as 'performance-related pay'). He eventually gave up, and described this model as 'the tragedy of education', and declared his sense of shame for being a party to it.

The comment of Sir Christopher Ball in the previous chapter, takes up where Holmes left off, and is worth repeating:
"The nation (and its governments of either persuasion) seems to be intent on reinforcing a failing system at present ... It is no use tinkering with our 19th-century model of education. It needs to be completely re-thought and restructured. Gradual reform is unlikely to succeed. Radical change is needed."

But not everyone is content to wait for governments to catch on and catch up. People at the grassroots, in a variety of countries, have been busy for the last twenty years or more. Two new books bear witness to this activity. The first is called, *Creating a Cooperative Learning Centre, an idea-book for home schooling families.* It is written by Katherine Houk from Chatham, New York, who is co-founder of the alternative learning centre, a co-operative which offers classes, workshops, field trips, and other adventures for families involved in home-based education. Her own children began to be educated at home in 1983. She is also involved in art and design, writing, and the ministry, especially interfaith work. Next, she is a director of the *Alliance for Parental Involvement in Education,* (ALLPIE), a non-profit organisation dedicated to providing education information to families.

She tells the story of a centre she co-founded along with a few dedicated parents, now serving over 70 children. In the process, the author provides ideas you can apply to your own situation. *"Discover how you can create a gathering place for creative and joyful learning in your community, a place for people of all ages,"* declares the author.

The sequence of events follows a now familiar pattern. After an often lengthy period of heart-searching, debate and enquiry, a family decides that the best option available to them is to educate at home. Apprehensively, they join the ranks of those reluctant heretics, the home-based educating families. Naturally, they have a concern about social life and social skills. So, first, they set out to find clubs and groups in the community to join, ranging from the Guides and Scouts to judo groups, choirs and craft groups.

Then they decide, often at the same time as searching for community groups, to make contact with other families who are educating at home, and see if they can do a few things together. If this is a success, the next stage is that these families may decide to meet on a more regular basis and rent premises for this to happen. In this way a co-operative learning centre is created.

Houk's book gives pages of practical advice to anyone wishing to follow the same path. There are sections on organisation and operation, laws and bylaws, contracts and agreements, finance, dealing with the press, planning the programme, and the strength and challenge of diversity.

In the UK too, groups have been developing the same kind of vision. *Human Scale Education* has supported the development of small parent run schools, known in the USA as charter schools. The newly-founded *Centre for Personalised Education Trust* has started work supporting, in particular, learning centres created by groups of home-educating families. A well established one is the *Otherwise Club* in London. Chris Shute reports, *"It meets twice a week in a sort of community hall in north London ... The club is a support group for home-schooling families. It does not do their job for them, but it provides a context in which they can meet together, discuss their problems and allow their children to do a little learning in company with other youngsters who are also being educated at home,"* (in Education Now *News and Review*, Summer 2000)

A newcomer to the scene is the *Learning Studio* at Bishops Castle in Shropshire, which is part of the Living Village Trust development. Carole Salmon reports: *"The learning studio is already functioning on a small scale on the ground floor of a house that the Trust owns next to the site. We are hoping to have a purpose-built building within 18 months. The idea here is a centre for home-educated children to meet, play and learn together."* (in *Natural Parent* Sept/Oct 2000, p.26)

The second book is entitled, *Creating Learning Communities: models, resources, and new ways of thinking about teaching and learning.* It is edited by Ron Miller of the Foundation for Educational Renewal Inc. USA. It is in all respects a contemporary book. First of all it was written and published on the Internet and may be inspected free at www. PathsofLearning.com. The writers met on the Internet on a list-serve, CCL-LLCs@onelist.com. The common interests of the writers were the future of learning and the potential impact on society of co-operative community lifelong learning centres. These are emerging particularly drawn from the rapidly growing home schooling movement. This social phenomena is spontaneously self-organising without leadership, without planning, without design and often without being noticed. All of the educators involved, whether home schoolers, autodidacts, co-operatives or futurists, are trying to transform the learning system.
In the book, thirty leading innovators and writers tackle the issue of the next learning system to replace the dying mass coercive schooling model. Contributors include Linda Dobson, Pat Farengo, Katherine Houk, Bill Ellis, Don Glines, Jerry Mintz, Ron Miller, and myself.

These writers are agreed that our common experience tells us that all is not well with society. Today's schools teach by the mode they use - hierarchy, self-interest, authoritarianism, patriarchy, competition, materialism, and survival of the fittest. Humanity looks set to destroy itself with this value system. And, increasing number of observers, including scientists, philosophers, historians, and artists, are starting to warn us, that if present trends continue, we are headed for an enormous cultural and ecological disaster.

Creating Learning Communities is a remarkable book that includes a number of inspiring case studies. There are also analyses of the age of information technology and its impact. A key section looks at the philosophical roots of the next learning system. Finally there is a directory of information and contacts.

The book sets us a challenge. Emerging is a future in which all people will be able to learn what and when they want, regardless of age - a future where learning can be lifelong, where the old paradigms are set aside. We will be able to roam intellectually and seek out as much knowledge, information, and experience as we wish, where we can both learn and teach according to our curiosity, needs, and knowledge. In most segments of society we are some distance from this future, not least because schooling, based on the 'tell them and test them' ideology has dimmed our imagination. But here and there, in growing numbers, all around the world, people are actually living this future today.

Ron Miller draws distinctions between three general approaches. A transmission approach assumes that the primary purpose of education is to induct young people into the established values, beliefs, and accepted knowledge of the existing society. The transaction approach is more sensitive to the social context of learning. There is more room for individual differences, more respect for diverse understandings, and a concern that only a democratic community encourages dialogue and experimentation. The transformational approach is more radical and proposes that to educate the human being is not merely to make the him a knowledgeable, productive member of society (transmission), an active, engaged citizen (transaction), but also to encourage each person to discover a deeper meaning for his or her life.

Miller adds the fourth possibility, self direction. It is found well expressed in the writings of John Holt and AS.Neill. It holds that we are naturally learners, and if social institutions would stop cluttering our paths with various prejudices, agendas, and bad habits, young people would follow a natural curriculum and learn throughout their lives of all that is necessary to experience meaningful and productive lives. Most, if not all, of the structures of schooling - grades, lesson plans, age groupings, teaching strategies, key stages and obsessive testing - are seen as irrelevant and counter-productive.

The writers in this book have little sympathy for the existing learning system of mass, coercive schooling.   Some see it as obsolete.   Well, perhaps spending time in a museum of education might not be all that harmful, you might argue, but some of the writers see mass schooling as actually counter-productive in producing a series of bad habits, ranging from intellectual, through emotional and psychological and political, to social. Others go further and see mass, coercive schooling as infringing three and sometimes four human rights.

One of these is conscription to an ageist institution.   Such an imposition is justified by the dubious belief that being compelled to spend large amounts of time in the company of people chosen for you and of the same age and immaturity as yourself, will somehow turn you into a mature human being. What is really does is set up the context for the tyranny of the peer group with its pressure on the inmates to conform to whatever fads and fashions grip it at any particular time, whether it be expensive trainers or expensive drugs.

The writers in this book have found common cause through the internet. In their own communities they can often be rather lone voices for a more sane learning system.   Now, they are able to avoid the gentle sensorship of the media using the technique of regular omission from consideration through the spiking of letters and articles by newspaper and magazine editors.   They can present their ideas direct to a world-wide audience. And curiously, some of the writers now report that they are being asked by those formerly using 'deaf-ear' tactics, to write some pieces for them.

Creating Learning Communities edited by Ron Miller, (Brandon VT: Foundation for Educational renewal, 2000, ISBN 1-885580-04-5) can be obtained from Educational Heretics Press, 113 Arundel Drive, Bramcote Hills, Nottingham NG9 3FQ at £19-50 p. & p. included)

Creating a Cooperative Learning Centre, an idea-book for home schooling families, by Katherine Houk, (Chatham NY: Longview,

2000, ISBN 0-9636096-3-7) is available from H.E.R.O books, 58 Portland Road, Hove, East Sussex, BN3 5DL at £12-50

Postscript:
The Boulevard of Broken Dreams

Almost everyone starts out with hopes and even high hopes of going to school. Children may anticipate entry into a world of interest, stimulation and development. Teachers may anticipate a worthwhile, satisfying and positive occupation. Parents may hope for the continued blossoming of their children. Grandparents may anticipate happy grand-children growing up positively in the world.

Yet teachers end up reporting that *"We are just miserable rule followers ..."* This is the verdict of a teacher in South Africa, reported by Clive Harber in *State of Transition*, London, Symposium Books, 2001. But it could be anywhere, given Edward de Bono's verdict that all the schooling systems he has encountered in the world are a disgrace. All the ones I have encountered are also a disgrace, although some are larger disasters than others.

Next, children aged six can already be reporting that they are aware that their minds are being highjacked. They recognise that their concerns, their interests, their agendas, are already being systematically squeezed off the agenda. But they feel powerless to do anything about it and are already, at six years of age, reconciled to having to conform to a script written by remote others. They, too, become 'just miserable rule-followers'. (see research by Ann Sherman in *Rules, Routines and Regimentation*, Nottingham: Educational Heretics Press, 1996.) A recent report in the *Guardian* newspaper, June 5th 2001, on *The School That I'd Like,* was a catalogue of suggestions from the inmates about how to make schools better. The report turned out to be a long plea by the children for the recognition of some of their interests and concerns, for some of them to be put back on the agenda and for some power to be returned to them.

Thirdly, parents may report that school is not doing the kind of things they had hoped. They may find they have handed their children over, in good faith, to a bunch of strangers, hoping for the best, but getting something undesirable. Some can take action and educate at home as a better option, others are forced by circumstances to become 'miserable rule-followers'. Some can try damage-limitation.

This is, in the words of the song title, *the 'Boulevard of Broken Dreams'*. High hopes gradually – and sometimes very suddenly – becoming shattered. Schooling may then become what has been sometimes been described as long-sentence of quiet suffering, endurance and low-level misery. Some learn to stand it better than others.

Congratulations must be offered to those teachers, and sometimes whole schools, who manage, despite the odds, to maintain some kind of oasis in the general desert. But it is the long tracts of desert with which I am concerned.

One of the propositions of this book is that this is a consequence of abandoning natural learning and the natural curriculum. In its place has been imposed false and shallow learning and the largely junk State curriculum.

We can stop all this. It has been pointed out many times that mass coercive schooling is NOT a fact of nature. Humans invented it about 150 years ago, and if it is no good, or has outlived any useful purpose, WE CAN SCRAP IT and devise learning arrangements and places that are convivial and far removed from places for miserable rule followers. Adapting the catch phrase of a popular TV series, 'we have the technology and know-how – we can redesign it'.

But we shall need a serious radical re-think to do this. Tinkering with an obsolete and counter-productive system will not do it. Returning to the principles of natural learning looks like a big step on the way forward.

Details of articles as published in *Natural Parent magazine*

Part one: Natural learning and the natural curriculum

1. 'Natural learners' was published in *Natural Parent* December 1997 under the title 'Your natural learner'.
2. 'Wanted! A new vocabulary for learning' was published in *Natural Parent* January/February 1999 under the title of 'New words for new learning'.
3. 'The natural curriculum' was published in *Natural Parent* March/April 2000 under the title of 'The natural curriculum'.

Part two: Parents

1. 'Reluctant educational heretics' was published in *Natural Parent* November 1997 under the title of 'A quiet revolution that begins in the home'.
2. 'Parents as researchers' was published in *Natural Parent* March 1988 under the title of 'Always searching'.
3. 'Purposive conversation and effective learning' was published in *Natural Parent* March/April 1999 under the title of 'Talk that's far from cheap'.
4. 'Damage limitation' was published in *Natural Parent* January/February 2000 under the title of 'How to survive school'
5. 'Grandparent power?' was published in *Natural Parent* July/August 2000 under the title of 'Grandparent power?'

Part three: Learners and learning systems

1. 'Order! Order!' was published in *Natural Parent* January 1988 under the title of 'Order! Order!'
2. 'Where does the bully mentality come from?' was published in *Natural Parent* June 1988 under the title of 'Where the bullying starts'.
3. 'Back to the future?' was published in *Natural Parent* May/June 1999 under the title of 'Putting children in their place'.
4. 'Its not what you learn but the way that you learn it' was published in *Natural Parent* September/October 2000 under the title of 'What sort of children do we want?'
5. 'Beans in a jar and the domination of the peer group' was published in *Natural Parent* March/April 2001 under the title of 'How many peers make five?'
6. 'Instead of fear' was published in *Natural Parent* May/June 2001 under the title of 'In place of fear'.

Part four: Teachers

1. 'What is a good teacher?'' was published in *Natural Parent* September/October 1998 was published under the title of 'What makes a good teacher?'
2. 'Crowd instruction: the cop without a uniform' was published in *Natural Parent* July 1998 under the title of 'The cop without a uniform'.
3. 'Head teachers, leadership and courage' was published in *Natural Parent* May/June 2000 was published under the title of 'What kind of head teacher do you want for your children?'

Part five: Superstitions and myths

1. 'The superstition of socialisation' was published in *Natural Parent* November/December 1998 under the title of 'A superstition called socialisation'.
2. 'The superstition of standards' was published in *Natural Parent* July/August 1999 under the title of 'How your child can be a deep learner'.
3. 'Some educational superstitions of our time - Shakespeare, Maths and Handwriting' was published in *Natural Parent* April 1998 under the title of 'The three myths'.
4. 'Dyslexia and the obsession with literacy' was published in *Natural Parent* February 1998 under the title of 'Tell it, don't spell it'.
5. 'You become what you read' was published in *Natural Parent* September/October 1999 under the title of 'The writing's on the wall'.

Part six: Visions of the next learning system

1. 'Teaching tomorrow' was published in *Natural Parent* November/December 2000 under the title of 'School's out'.
2. 'Roland Meighan interviews Sir Christopher Ball' was published in *Natural Parent* November/December 1999 under the title of 'The key to true learning'.
3. 'Learning centres instead of schools?' was published in *Natural Parent* January/February 2001 under the title of 'Parents are doing it for themselves'.

Natural Parent

A subscription for 12 issues is £25-95. *Natural Parent* is published six times a year.
Send to: *Natural Parent* Subscription Dept., Tower House, Sovereign Park, Market Harborough, Leics LE16 9EF (Telephone 01858 438 894)

Some useful contacts

Education Otherwise is the largest home-based education self-help group in UK. For information, send an A5 size stamped addressed envelope to:

P.O.Box 7420, London N9 9SG
Helpline: 0870 7300074
www/education-otherwise.org

Home Education Advisory Service (HEAS) provides information, advice and support for home-educating families at P.O.Box 98, Welwyn Garden City, Herts AL8 6AN   Telephone 01707 371 854

. www.heas.org.uk

See also:

www.home-education/org.uk	www.home-ed/org
www.edheretics/gn.apc.org	www.educationnow/gn.apc.org
www.free-range-education/co.uk	www.schoolhouse/org.uk

Some further reading

Ask for *the Educational Heretics Press* catalogue from:
113 Arundel Drive, Bramcote Hills, Nottingham NG9 3FQ
(Tel/fax 0115 925 7261)   for details of titles such as:

The Holistic Educators by Cara Martin

John Holt: Personalised Education and the Reconstruction of Schooling by Roland Meighan

Without Boundaries by Jan Fortune-Wood

Rules, Routines and Regimentation by Ann Sherman

Compulsory Schooling Disease by Chris Shute

Creating Learning Communities edited by Bill Ellis